So You Want to Be Rich

Herbert N. Weisman, D.D.S., CFP

A Hearthstone Book

Carlton Press Corp ❖ New York, NY

Effective May 1, 1995, the United States Treasury will no longer guarantee the floor interest rate on EE savings bonds. Further, the rate is no longer tied to five-year U.S. Treasury notes. Instead, it is tied to ninety-day Treasury bills. This results in a lower yield.

Copyright © 1995 by Herbert N. Weisman
ALL RIGHTS RESERVED
Manufactured in the United States of America
ISBN 0-8062-4965-X

*To my wife Dori
and my children,
David and Marnee*

Member:
American Dental Association and affiliated state and local organizations, Academy of General Dentistry, Institute of Certified Financial Planners, Registry of Certified Financial Planners, Fellow, Royal Society of Health (England), Israel Dental Association Alpha Omega Dental Fraternity

Non-related Organizations:
American Radio Relay League, Biblical Archaeology Society, United States Aikido Association, Masons, other civic organizations, Marquis' *Who's Who In the Upper Midwest*, 24th ed.

Contents

Introduction ix
1. What Is Financial Planning? 1
   Financial Planning Defined
   Reasons for Not Doing Financial Planning
   Costs of Failure to Plan
   The Financial Planning Process
2. Getting Out of Debt 14
   Some Personal Planning Observations
3. Protection: an Insurance Overview 17
   Basis of Claims Payment
   Ways to Reduce Premium Cost
4. Life Insurance 20
   A Brief History
   Uses
   Important Considerations
   Policy Provisions
   Riders to Individual Life Insurance Policies
   Kinds of Life Insurance
   How Much Life Insurance Is Needed?
5. Property and Casualty Insurance 29
   An Overview
6. Homeowner's Insurance 31
   Uses and Provisions

7. Personal Automobile Policy 35
   An Overview
   Financial Responsibility Laws
   Personal Automobile Policy Format
   Medical Payments
   Uninsured Motorist
   Underinsured Motorist
   Duties of the Insured
8. Liability Insurance 41
9. Health Insurance 43
   An Overview
10. Disability Income Insurance 45
    Overhead Expense Policies
    Medical Expense Policies
    Medicare
    Medicare (Part A, 1995)
    Medicare (Part B, 1995)
11. Long-Term Care Policies 52
12. Savings 56
13. Retirement Planning 60
    Cost of Retirement
14. Sources of Retirement Income 64
15. Pension Plans 70
    Kinds of Retirement Plans (Tax-Favored)
    Pension Plan Specifications
16. Nonqualified Deferred Compensation Plans 84
17. Managing Assets During Retirement 87
    Portfolio Management
    Asset Allocation
    Common Pitfalls
18. Investments 93
    Risks Associated with Investments
    Rules for Successful Investing
    The business Cycle
19. Investment Vehicles 102
    Common Stocks
    Preferred Stock
    Bonds
    Deep Discount Bonds and Zero Coupon Bonds

     Kinds of Municipal Bonds
     Other Important Information
     Bond Funds
     Other Fixed Income Obligations
     Real Estate Investment Trusts (REITS)
     Other Forms of Real Estate Investments
     Oil and Gas Ventures
     Put and Call Options
     Commodity Futures Trading
     Collectibles
     Mutual Funds
     Limited Partnerships
     Treasury Securities
20. Common Concerns 121
     Financing College Education
     How to Increase Your Income in a Low-Interest Environment
     Charitable Giving
     Types of Contributions
     Divorce Planning
     Weathering the Storm—Natural and Man-Made
21. Estate Planning, Wills and Trusts 136
     Introduction to Estate Planning
     Probate
     Wills
     Joint Ownership
     Trusts
     Power of Attorney
     Life Insurance Revisited
     Living Will
     Letter of Instruction
     Managing Property of Minors
     Unified Federal Gift and Estate Tax
     Common Estate Planning Mistakes

Introduction

Studies by the Savings and Loan Associations over the years have demonstrated that the average person, after working 40 or more years, has little to show for it. In fact, only 20 percent of the people who reach retirement age can afford to do so without working. Why is this so? One reason is that we Americans have gotten used to the idea that we should "live for today." We have the lowest savings rate of any industrialized nation in the world. Another reason may be that we have come to expect that someone else (e.g., our employer or Social Security) will provide for us during our "old age." Perhaps the most compelling reason is that most people have not been taught the basics of the financial planning process: insurance, investing, and estate planning.

In this book these concepts will be discussed in some detail. Where possible, a checklist or table is provided to help the reader evaluate his or her own situation. Don't hesitate to check with your tax advisor before implementing any of the concepts discussed.

At this point I should like to thank my wife, Dori, and my children, David and Marnee, for putting up with my obsession with regard to writing this book.

1 What Is Financial Planning?

❧

Several years ago, two old friends got together for lunch one day. It had been twenty-five years since they had graduated from high school. Let us call them Joe and Charley.

Joe appeared to be very successful. Charley was less so. As they were having lunch, Charley said to Joe, "Joe, what is the secret of your success? Everything you touch seems to turn to gold." Joe replied, "I have my ups and downs like everyone else. When I feel down I go home and get out my Bible. I then put my finger into my Bible. Whatever word my finger touches is what I do. Last time I felt depressed, I got my Bible and put my finger into it. When I opened it up I saw that I was touching the word 'gold.' So I invested in gold. It went up a lot so I sold it and made a bundle." "That's a good idea," replied Charley, "I think that I will try that."

Charley went home, got out his Bible, and put his finger into it. When he opened it up to find which word his finger was touching, he was surprised. It read "Chapter 11"—bankruptcy.

The point of this story is that financial planning cannot be left to chance. It must be done in a careful and thoughtful manner. It should be reviewed on a semiannual basis or whenever major changes occur in a person's life. Examples of these are marriage, divorce, inheritances, etc.

Financial Planning Defined

What is personal financial planning? Personal financial planning may be described as a controlled, disciplined approach to defining one's financial objectives and establishing a plan of how to achieve them. These goals may include getting out of debt by a certain date, buying a house, putting aside money for a child's college education, or planning for retirement.

Reasons for Not Doing Financial Planning

Many people do not do personal financial planning for any number of reasons. Some people feel that they are already doing everything "right" without having a written formal plan. They fail to realize that a written plan shows where people are strong and where they are weak. As an example, financial planners often find that many people have an adequate amount of life insurance but do not have any disability insurance. Statistics show that for a thirty-two-year-old man, the odds of having a serious injury before age sixty-five are six to one. "Serious" is defined as being out of work for ninety days or more. How important would this be to a dentist or physician who was seriously injured? Others procrastinate because they are "too busy." Some individuals resent paying for the cost of planning services. Still other people delay planning because they cannot bear the thought of illness or death.

Costs of Failure to Plan

While it may be understandable, from the human point of view, why people fail to plan, the costs may be high. In the event of catastrophe, an unprotected or inadequately protected person or family may lose many of their assets. This may be particularly evident in situations such as automobile accidents, disability, unemployment, prolonged illness, or death.

An individual without a will may not have his possessions distributed to whom he/she would like to receive them. Further, where large estates exist, failure to plan may result in larger estate taxes or gift taxes.

Another instance where lack of planning can create unnecessary hardship is where there is a closely held family business. Failure to plan for future disposition can result in severe problems in the event of premature death, disability, or retirement of one of the owners. Aside from tax-related problems, family discord may result.

Probably the most important reason to plan is to achieve your personal objectives. Failure to do so may result in inadequate retirement income or having to force your family to accept a lower standard of living.

THE FINANCIAL PLANNING PROCESS

The financial planning process has six steps. They are:

(1) Gathering information
(2) Establishing goals and objectives
(3) Determining working parameters
(4) Establishing a plan and an alternative plan
(5) Implementing the plan
(6) Monitoring the plan

Let us look at the six steps in more detail. The first step is gathering information. This step is straightforward. The individual lists all his/her assets and liabilities. This determines the person's "net worth." (An example of this and other forms is at the end of the chapter.) A "cash flow" statement should be made showing the family's income from all sources and outflows for at least one month. Banks usually require both of the above statements for a one-year period. Beside financial information, personal feelings regarding risk tolerance, time horizons, and relationships should be defined. For example, the handling of future care and maintenance of a divorced spouse may cause strong emotions. A thorough review should be made of all insurance policies (life, property, health, and casualty and liability) to determine current status. Wills, trusts, employee benefits, Social Security benefits, and tax situations should be reviewed.

The second step of the financial planning process is establishing goals and objectives. It is not enough to say "I want to be rich." This is a wish. In order for it to be a goal it must be a specific objective, achieveable in a definite period. The focus here for most people might be as follows:

1.1 Personal Risk Protection

    2.1 Premature Death
    2.2 Disability Income Losses
    2.3 Medical Care Expenses
    2.4 Property and Liability Losses
    2.5 Unemployment

1.2 Capital Accumulation for

    2.1 Emergency Fund Purposes
    2.2 Family Purposes
    2.3 General Investment Portfolio
    2.4 Retirement Income
    2.5 Reduction of Tax Burden
        3.1   During Lifetime
        3.2   Death
    2.6 Estate Planning
    2.7 Investment and Property Management

It should be pointed out that it may be necessary to seek expert advice to decide what is adequate for each person's needs. Too often people are reluctant to pay for professional advice because they feel it is expensive. It can be more expensive if you try to do everything yourself. No one can be an expert on everything. If your professional does not perform, you may have recourse. If *you* foul up, you may lose everything.

The third step in the planning process is determining your parameters. In simple terms, you look at your present position in light of what you are trying to accomplish. There are usually some problems that need to be solved. Under the guidance of advisers, you can often find alternatives to meet your objectives within the personal and financial constraints imposed.

At the fourth stage of the planning process, the aforementioned information is reviewed, and a plan and/or alternative plan is developed. Sometimes it is necessary for a person to change to a more realistic perspective. Other times plans have to be modified or put on hold until a sound foundation can be built. Remember, reasonable people may disagree on the best way for you to reach your objectives.

The fifth stage of the planning process is implementing your plan. It doesn't benefit anyone if the plan is not acted upon. Too often people delay implementing the chosen plan because they feel uncomfortable with the recommendations either in the plan or the investments suggested. If you don't feel comfortable with either, be sure to discuss these feelings with your adviser. It goes without saying that you can reject those parts of a plan with which you do not agree or that you do not feel you can afford.

Finally, as with any major investment, be sure to monitor your progress at least every six months. Remember, the "plan" is not cast in stone. Circumstances change in everyone's life. Often some fine tuning is required.

Checklists:

The following checklists are provided as a guide to help you organize your assets. They are not necessarily complete. Each person should use them with his financial adviser and modify them where needed.

A list of "Whom to Call" if premature death should occur is also given.

Statement of Net Worth for

_____

Date_____

Assets
Liquid Assets
  Cash and checking accounts   _____
  Savings account(s)   _____
  Money market funds   _____
  Life insurance cash values   _____
  U.S. Savings bonds   _____
  Brokerage accounts   _____
  Other   _____
    Total liquid assets   _____
Marketable Investments
  Common stocks   _____
  Mutual funds   _____
  Corporate bonds   _____
  Municipal bonds   _____
  Certificates of deposit   _____
  Other   _____
    Total marketable investments   _____
Nonmarketable Investments
  Business interests   _____
  Investment real estate   _____
  Pension accounts   _____
  Profitsharing accounts   _____
  Thrift plan accounts   _____
  IRA and other retirement accounts   _____
  Tax sheltered investments   _____
  Other   _____
    Total nonmarketable investments   _____
Personal Real Estate
  Residence   _____
  Vacation home   _____
    Total personal real estate   _____

Other Personal Assets
   Auto(s) _____
   Boat(s) _____
   Furs and jewelry _____
   Collections, hobbies, etc. _____
   Furniture and household
     accessories _____
    Total other personal assets _____
      Total _____

Liabilities and Net Worth
Current Liabilities
   Charge accounts, credit card
    charges, and other bills payable _____

   Installment credit and other short-term loans _____

   Unusual tax liabilities _____
    Total current liabilities _____
Long-term Liabilities
   Mortgage notes on personal
     real estate _____
   Mortgage notes on investment
     real estate _____
   Margin loans _____
Life insurance policy loans _____
Other _____
   Total long-term liabilities _____
    Total liabilities _____
    Family net worth _____
    Total family liabilities and
     net worth _____

Family Income Statement

Income
Salaries
  You   _____
  Your Spouse   _____
  Others   _____
    Total Salaries   _____
Investment Income
  Interest (taxable)   _____
  Interest (nontaxable)   _____
  Dividends   _____
  Real estate   _____
  Realized capital gains   _____
  Other investment income   _____
    Total investment income   _____
Bonuses, Profitsharing Payments, Etc.   _____
Other Income   _____
    Total income   _____
Expenses and Fixed Obligations
Ordinary Living Expenses   _____
Interest Expense
  Consumer loans   _____
  Bank loans   _____
  Mortgage notes   _____
  Insurance policy loans   _____
  Other interest   _____
    Total interest expense   _____
Debt Amortization (mortgage, notes, consumer debt, etc.)   _____
Insurance Premiums
  Life insurance   _____
  Health insurance   _____
  Property and liability   _____
    Total insurance premiums   _____
Charitable Contributions   _____
Tuition and educational expense   _____
Payments for support of aged parents or other dependents   _____

Taxes:
  Federal income tax   _____
  State (and city) income tax   _____
  Social Security tax   _____
  Local property taxes   _____
  Other taxes   _____
    Total taxes   _____
      Total expenses and fixed
        obligations   _____
Balance Available for Discretionary Investment _____

Checklist of Priorities

1. Make a will
2. Adequate insurance (life, health, disability, malpractice, income replacement, etc.)
3. Emergency cash reserve (3–6 months reserve)
4. House with mortgage (not applicable to older people)
5. Debt elimination
6. Quality common stocks, mutual funds, etc., for liquidity
7. Other conventional investments (bonds, real estate, etc.)
8. Tax shelters (Tread carefully. Many people buy these to save taxes. Investments should be made based on their rate of return—regardless of the tax savings.)
9. Speculation (This should be limited to 10 percent of total assets.)

References

CFP I Study Guide, College for Financial Planning, Denver, Colo., 1992

Personal Financial Planning, third edition; Hallman, G. Victor, Rosenbloom, Jerry S.; McGraw-Hill; New York, N.Y., 1985

Weisman, Herbert N., D.D.S., "Personal Money Management for Dentists," *North West Dentistry*, pp. 135–137, March-April, 1974

Wolf, Harold A., Personal Financial Planning, Alternate 8th edition, Allyn & Bacon/Ginn Press, Austin, Texas, 1991

Whom to Call

Accountant
Name _____
Address _____
Telephone _____

Attorney
Name _____
Address _____
Telephone _____

Bank
Name _____
Address _____
Telephone _____
Checking Account No. _____
Savings Account No. _____

Bank
Name _____
Address _____
Telephone _____
Mortgage No. _____
Loan No. _____

Broker
Name _____
Company _____
Address _____
Telephone _____
Account No. _____

Financial Planner _____
Name _____
Company _____
Address _____
Telephone _____

Financial Products _____

Financial Products continued

_____
_____

Insurance Agents
Home Insurance
Name _____
Address _____
Telephone _____

Life Insurance
Name _____
Address _____
Telephone _____

Health Insurance
Name _____
Address _____
Telephone _____

Automobile Insurance
Name _____
Address _____
Telephone _____

Business Insurance
Name _____
Address _____
Telephone _____

Clergy
Name _____
Address _____
Telephone _____

Safe Deposit Box (Do NOT keep will in Safe Deposit Box)
Bank _____
Box No. _____

Key Location _____
Bank Address _____
Telephone _____
Contents
    _____
    _____
    _____
    _____

Living Will (if available)
Location _____

Credit Cards
Name _____
Account No. _____
Address _____

Name _____
Account No. _____
Address _____

Name _____
Account No. _____
Address _____

Name _____
Account No. _____
Address _____

Other Important Information
_____
_____
_____

Planning Questions to Consider
1. Where am I now in terms of net worth? Monthly cash flow?
2. Is there any discretionary income left over to implement a financial plan?

3. What are my short-term goals? (These may include getting out of debt, planning for children's education, retirement planning, divorce planning, etc.)
4. What are my intermediate goals? Long-term goals?
5. What kind of life style do I want? Can I afford it?
6. Where do I want to live? This may include climate factors, tax factors, decisions to own or rent your home, etc.
7. Do I have family members or relatives with special needs that must be provided for?
8. If I should die, will my family be able to care for their needs adequately?
9. Do I have enough disability insurance in case I can't work? How about adequate medical insurance?
10. Can I afford to retire? If so, how many years of retirement should I plan for? What about inflation? Will I have enough purchasing power to live a comfortable life style?
11. What sacrifices am I willing to make to accomplish my goals?

2 Getting Out of Debt

In the previous chapter the financial planning process was discussed. You probably think that this is good for someone else who has assets. Further, that you can barely make ends meet from paycheck to paycheck. The plan suggested in this chapter comes from George Clason's book *The Richest Man in Babylon* (Hawthorn Books, Inc., New York, N.Y.). Though simple in nature, it is highly effective.

First, you should be aware of some realities of credit and debt. If used wisely, they are a strong financial planning tool. If abused, they can doom you to a life of poverty. The first reality is this: BANKS WILL NOT LEND MONEY TO PEOPLE WHO DO NOT HAVE ANY (OR AT LEAST AN ASSET OF VALUE). The logic of this is simple. They want assurances that they will be repaid.

The second reality that you should be aware is "The Law of TINSTAAFL." This states that "there is no such thing as a free lunch." This is particularly true with the use of "plastic money," or credit cards. The banks that issue them charge 12 percent to 19 percent on the average daily balances for the privilege of using them. (That is, if you cannot pay the full balance each month). Can you afford to give away one eighth to one fifth of your income each month? If you are compulsive about using credit cards, try putting them in a drawer. Use them only for purchasing major items or in emergencies.

Now to the plan for getting out of debt. The first rule is: *Pay yourself first.* Put aside 10 percent of your paycheck into a savings account. Most planners believe that a person should have three to six months income in reserve for emergencies. My personal feeling is that it should be three to four months income. Amounts over this should be set aside on a regular basis for investments. When you think about it, the after-tax return on a daily interest savings account does not keep up with inflation. Believe it or not, you will find that you will live just as well on 10 percent less.

The second rule for getting out of debt is: *Assign 20 percent of your check for paying your bills.* Let all your vendors know that you are trying to clear up all your bills and how much you intend to send them each month. As the smaller bills clear, you will be able to send more to the larger accounts. Your vendors will be happier than if you try to pay them in a haphazard manner.

The third rule for clearing your debts is: *Live on the other 70 percent.* It is important that you sit down with your spouse and figure out your real needs. Many people confuse their wants with their needs. The family cash flow statement at the end of the previous chapter will be most helpful to sort this out. The beautiful thing about this plan is that after all your bills are paid, you end up living on 90 percent of your income. Just remember *not* to charge more than 20 percent of your income each month.

SOME PERSONAL PLANNING OBSERVATIONS

Often, when two or more people in a family are working, they have a single joint checking account. This is strongly discouraged. All too often, when both people write checks from the same account, somebody forgets to record one. This leads to a strife regarding who forgot to do it. Though not opposed to joint checking and savings accounts, it is better for each person to have his own. (The joint feature can then be used with the other person's knowledge in case of emergency.)

Another common situation is a single family income with a non-working spouse. The income earner pays all the bills. The non-earner acquiesces—willingly or not. This is not a healthy situation for two reasons. First, the non-earner seldom knows the "real" income of the earner, so fights over money can result. Second, if the earner should die prematurely, the non-earner is left with little or no experience handling money. Insurance company statistics reveal that many people who inherit or receive large sums of unearned money lose it all within two years. It is much better for a couple to have separate checking accounts.

A third scenario occurs where there is a large family income from either one or two sources and a single joint checking account. This can work if both people are tolerant of mistakes and omissions by the other party. Experience has taught us that the first example is the most flexible and workable.

In most financial planning books this is usually not discussed. My observation is that checkbook misuse is a major source of debt.

3 Protection: an Insurance Overview

There are many kinds of insurance. There is insurance backed by the government, such as FHA insurance, GI insurance, and flood insurance. There is social insurance. Social Security and welfare entitlement programs are examples of this. Lastly, there is private insurance. Health, life, and casualty insurance are examples of this. In this chapter the basic underlying principles of insurance will be discussed. In subsequent chapters each form of private insurance will be discussed in detail.

What is insurance? Insurance is protection against **catastrophic** loss. It works because of the "Law of Large Numbers." This states that in a large homogeneous group, the probability of an event happening to any one person in the group (at a given time) is small. In essence, the many are helping the few, or the one, who may be experiencing unfortunate circumstances.

Basis of Claims Payment

Before an insurance company will pay a claim, it must decide that the claim was "accidental or fortuitous." Further, the loss must be measurable. Often, an insurance company will pay up to the maximums of the policy, but it does not cover the entire loss.

Frequently, people are underinsured. For instance, an individual buys a new home. The homeowner buys the correct amount of insurance. Time passes. The insured does not increase insurance annually to "keep up" with inflation. Years pass, and a fire occurs. The house burns down. Because he has not increased insurance, he receives only part of the replacement cost of the house. Most homeowner policies require carrying insurance equal to at least 80 percent of the fair market value of the property.

Ways to Reduce Premium Cost

With the potential for so many different kinds of losses, what can the individual do to minimize the cost of insurance premiums? There are five approaches that can reduce expense. First, the person can **avoid risk.** A situation in which this might happen might be the following: As a general practitioner (dentist) you may not feel comfortable removing impacted wisdom teeth. So you refer your patient to an oral surgeon. In this way you avoid the risk of hurting your patient. Specialists pay higher insurance premiums because they are willing to assume a greater risk.

A second means of reducing premiums is to **self-insure.** Due to the high cost of liability insurance many people choose to go "barefoot." This is foolhardy because eventually some event will occur to put them at risk.

A third means of minimizing losses (but not necessarily the cost of insurance) is to **transfer risk.** If you are willing to pay a large enough premium, an insurance company might be found to cover your potential loss. Sometimes a consortium of insurance companies will insure a large risk. An example of this is Lloyds of London. This is a group of over 2,250 different insurance companies. When a risk is large (for example, the space shuttle), individual members bid for a part of the action. Do you recognize the "Law of Large Numbers" again?

Another way to reduce premiums is by **sharing the risks.** This is done in several ways. The first way to do this is to increase the deductible. Look at the difference in premium for a single, non-smoking, adult male, 35 years old. The premium for a major medical policy with a $150 deductible is $1000.32. (This is without a co-deductible.) The premium for the same policy with a $1,000 deductible is $418.08. Note the considerable savings. The same principle applies to automobile insurance, property insurance, casualty insurance, malpractice insurance, etc. (Now, you begin to see the importance of having three months income in reserve for emergencies. It is a way to save money.)

Another means to reduce premium is to **increase the waiting time** before the insurance company has to pay the claim. This is most evident in accident and office overhead expense policies. If you can afford to wait thirty or sixty days before receiving benefits, the premium decreases substantially. Many companies offer even more extended waiting periods.

The last way of sharing risk is to **increase the "breakpoint."** This is the point where the insurance company begins to pay for 100 percent of the risk. The area between the deductible and the "breakpoint" is called the co-deductible. Usually, the patient pays 20 percent and the company pays 80 percent.

A final means of reducing premiums is to get a group policy. Again, because of the "Law of Large Numbers" premiums may be less than for individual policies. For people who may be considered "high risk," it is a way to get some small coverage at a reasonable cost.

4 Life Insurance

A Brief History

It appears that the first life insurance policy was issued in London, England, on June 18, 1536. It was a term insurance policy for one year to a William Gybbons. The amount was for 400 pounds. It was issued by a group of marine underwriters. Gybbons died within the year, and the group had to pay his heirs.

Other attempts were made to form insurance companies, but it wasn't until 1699 that the first "modern" life insurance company was formed. It was called the Society of Assurance of Widows and Orphans, and was based in London. It charged the same premiums to everyone.

In the United States in the mid-1700s, there were several attempts to start life insurance companies. Finally, in 1835, the first mutual life insurance company began. It was New England Life and still survives today. The previous chapter stated that the purpose of insurance was to protect against catastrophe. Such a catastrophe occurred in 1835. In that year a large fire broke out in New York City. The payment of claims from the Chicago fire, made famous by Mrs. O'Leary's cow, in 1871, and the San Francisco earthquake of 1906, ruined many insurance companies.

As you can imagine, the Great Depression of the 1930s was also hard on life insurance companies. Since World War II the industry has expanded and prospered.

USES

Life insurance can be used for many purposes. Its uses are only limited by your imagination. Some common situations in which life insurance is purchased are as follows: to help supplement family income in case of death of the "breadwinner"; to provide for children's future education; to provide for final expenses; to help pay estate taxes; to provide funds for partnership buyout at the death of one of the partners; to provide collateral for a loan; or to create an estate.

IMPORTANT CONSIDERATIONS

When buying life insurance there are several things of which to be aware. The first is that **the policy does NOT go into effect until the insurer (or his agent) receives the premium and issues a binder receipt.** The importance of this cannot be overemphasized. There have been many instances where an individual may have filled out the application for life insurance, turned it in with a check, and believed that he/she has made claim. Because the insurance company has not notified the person (by binder) that they accept, no contract exists. Therefore, the insurance company does not have to pay the claim.

Another important consideration is that **life insurance proceeds may be exempt from creditors.** Consider a situation in which a professional has a large amount of cash value life insurance. This asset is exempt from attachment in the case of suit, divorce, or bankruptcy.

Still another factor to consider is that **life insurance is not an indemnity.** That is, it does not attempt to restore a financial position that previously existed. It pays only the face value of the policy and sometimes double indemnity in the case of accidental death.

It should be noted that **a life insurance policy is considered property.** This means that it can be assigned to a third party. If the insured owns the policy, it is usually considered part of the person's gross estate. This means that it is taxable for estate tax purposes. (Sometimes it is better for another family member to own the policy. Though they also may be the beneficiary, they can avoid estate taxes on the policy.)

Finally, the owner can designate the beneficiary. So the insured can control who will ultimately benefit.

Policy Provisions

Occasionally, all of us get forgetful. Fortunately, insurance companies realize this. In order to protect the insured against lapses in coverage, **most life insurance policies have a 30-day grace period.**

Another policy provision is that **after a certain period, the insurance policy cannot be contested by the insurance company.** Though it may vary from policy to policy, most policies have a two-year provision. This means that even if there is concealment, misstatement, error, or even fraud, the company is obligated to pay any claim made against that policy. If the "error" is discovered by the company within two years, it will usually refund the premium paid to the insured and cancel the policy.

If a person should commit **suicide** within two years of taking a life insurance policy, the company will use the two-year means test and return the premium to the insured or his estate. This provision was instituted during the Great Depression. At that time some people would take out a policy and then commit suicide. In this way they thought they would be financially caring for their family. How ironic that they didn't read their policy.

Speaking of the Great Depression, another policy provision from that time allows the **insurance company to delay payment of the cash value of the policy for up to six months.**

This is only exercised during the most severe economic climate.

Another policy provision frequently found is **reinstatement of a policy after it has lapsed.** If the insured is still in good health and pays back premiums plus interest, the policy may be reinstated for up to three years.

Policy loans are allowed by insurance companies for "cash value" life insurance policies. The policy owner may borrow up to 90 or 95 percent of the cash value of the policy and still keep the policy in effect. Terms and rate of interest are stated in the policy. Frequently, this rate is lower than rates currently available at banks. As long as interest is paid, there is little pressure to repay the principal of the debt. One caveat—when this is done the face value of the policy is reduced by the amount borrowed in the event of death.

Though most policies do not include it, an insured may request a clause allowing for **automatic payment of the premium** from the cash reserves if the policyholder should fail to do so. With universal life and variable universal life policies, this is usually allowed.

For many years, life insurance companies did not pay claims if a person died in an aircraft accident. The **aviation exclusion clause** not only applies to military aircraft, but to hobby aviation as well. People who are in the reserves should be aware of this provision. Related to this, policyholders should be aware that there may be a **limited payoff in time of war.**

Nonforfeiture options are available for the policyholder who has accumulated value but wishes to stop making payments. One choice he/she can make is to **take the cash surrender value** of the policy. As an alternative he/she may **take a reduced paid up life insurance** policy. If this is done, more cash value insurance may be purchased from the annual dividends the policy pays, so there is no additional out-of-pocket expense. The third choice is to **use the dividends to purchase additional extended term insurance.**

The final policy options found in life insurance policies are known as **settlement options.** At the time that the policy is taken out, or at any later time, the policyholder can designate how he/she wants the beneficiaries paid.

Some individuals opt for a **lump sum payment.** Others choose to have their beneficiaries **receive a guaranteed amount for a fixed period.** This may be for any number of years. It is most valuable when the main consideration is to have a regular income during a certain period (e.g., during the child-rearing years). Still others may choose to have the company **pay to a beneficiary only the interest** from a policy. This is used when there are other sources of income available, so the principal is not currently needed. Finally, there are several **life income options.**

The first of these is **life income with period certain.** Under this option the payments to the insured are guaranteed for life. A minimum number of payments are guaranteed. If the insured dies before these are paid, a contingent beneficiary receives the payments for the period certain.

The second of these is **life income with refund.** Using this option the beneficiary receives the income for life. If he dies prematurely, the contingent beneficiary receives the income until the difference in proceeds between the original policy and the amount paid to the original beneficiary are used up. This may be in the form of an installment refund or in a cash lump sum.

The **joint and survivor income** option provides income to a couple at a certain level while both are alive. When the first recipient dies, the remaining one continues to receive the income at a somewhat reduced level. This is usually at one-half to two-thirds the previous level.

RIDERS TO INDIVIDUAL LIFE INSURANCE POLICIES

Before discussing the different types of life insurance policies, one should be aware of several riders that may be added to the policies that can enhance their value for relatively little additional cost. The first is called **guaranteed insurability.** This allows the policyholder to purchase additional insurance at various intervals without providing evidence of insurability. Another popular policy rider is known as **accidental**

death benefit. This may pay two or three times the face value of the policy due to accidental death. A third rider that is offered is **waiver of premium.** For payment of an extra premium, the premium may be waived for total disability. For partial disability, a **disability income** rider is available whereby income can be paid for a limited period. Not all companies offer this, so if this is important check with your agent.

KINDS OF LIFE INSURANCE

There are two broad categories of life insurance. They are **term** and **cash value.** Term insurance offers protection only. For young to middle-age people it offers the greatest protection per dollar. Term insurance comes in two forms. They are **level term** and **reducing term.**

For **level term insurance,** the face value of the policy remains the same during the "term" of the policy. The premium stays the same too. These policies are usually issued for one- to five-year periods. After that period the insurance coverage ceases. Many of these term policies have an option to renew, but at a higher premium. This is because as a person gets older, there is a greater chance of death.

The other kind of term insurance is known as **reducing term.** With this form of term insurance the premium remains level during the term of the policy, but the face value of the policy decreases at a rate of 3 to 5 percent per year. This kind of term insurance is used to guarantee loans in premature death. Banks frequently add the cost of this to a loan when lending money. (If you have another life insurance policy or another asset that you are willing to pledge for collateral, you may save yourself some money.)

The other category of life insurance is known as **cash value** or **permanent** insurance. It is so called because the premiums are permanently fixed while the policy is "in force." While part of the premium pays for protection, the other part builds up an interest-bearing, tax-deferred account. There are many variations of this idea. The most common are as follows:

Whole life (straight life) insurance has a fixed premium. The policy runs to age one hundred and ceases. Then the policyholder gets the face value of the policy. An insured may borrow up to 95 percent or the cash value of the policy and still keep it "in force." If the person should die while the loan is outstanding, his beneficiary would receive the face value of the policy minus the amount of the loan. The loan is repaid at the convenience of the policyholder.

Endowment policies combine enforced savings with term insurance. The insurance is for a fixed period (e.g., twenty years). After that period the individual gets the face value of the policy and insurance ceases. This type of policy has not been very popular since the tax reform act of 1986. The reason is that a capital gains tax must be paid on the deferred income generated by the policy, but this still might be a good way to shelter some assets from creditors.

Modified whole life insurance is a hybrid of the two kinds of insurance previously discussed. Here the premium is for a fixed period, but the insurance continues. In essence, this is paid-up insurance.

Universal insurance uses the cash reserves to pay for term insurance. The premium and the face value are flexible. Since there is enough money in the reserves to pay the next month's premium the policy remains "in force." So if the policyholder cannot temporarily pay his premium for whatever reason, he/she will not lose his coverage. The insurance company must make full disclosure of how much of the premium is for insurance and how much is for cash value. With this type of policy the cash reserves are invested in U.S. Government securities.

Variable insurance has a fixed premium. Unlike the other forms of "cash value" insurance, the policyholder can decide how the cash reserves are invested (within certain guidelines). The company gives the policy owner a choice between money market funds, bond funds, and different types of equity funds. It is like putting your money into a family of mutual funds under an insurance umbrella. In that way, any gains are tax deferred. In exchange for this privilege the policy owner gives up the right of guaranteed cash value for the possibility of having a greater death benefit. Originally, there was a possibility of a death benefit of less than the face value. Now, most insurance companies will guarantee the face amount of the policy.

Juvenile insurance is basically an endowment policy to pay for a child's future education.

How Much Life Insurance is Needed?

In spite of what many insurance agents tell you, there is no "rule of thumb." There are some things to consider. Each person is different. Consider, for example: What are you liabilities? What will your final expenses be? (This might include funeral expense, administrative costs, probate, etc.) Special needs should be considered (e.g., children's college education and emergency funds). Another need might be to provide sufficient income to allow a family to make a gradual readjustment in living standards. In this same vein, enough income must be provided for the family until the children are self-sufficient and for the widow(er) after they leave home. Further, life insurance cash values can be converted to provide income during retirement.

So how much life insurance do you need? The answer is that each person needs to review existing assets to figure out if they can satisfy the above needs. (Don't forget to consider Social Security income and other family sources of income. This is not available to the surviving spouse if the children are over fifteen years old and/or the spouse is under sixty.) After reviewing what assets are available, determining how much insurance will be needed should be somewhat easy.

Life Insurance Checklist

Type of life insurance policy _____
Policyholder _____
Date issued _____
Face amount ($) _____
Current cash value ($) _____
Annual premium ($) _____
Participation / Nonparticipation _____
Outstanding loan ($) _____
Loan interest rate (%) _____
Payer _____
Primary beneficiary _____
Contingent beneficiary _____

5 Property and Casualty Insurance

An Overview

In the previous chapter we saw that life insurance is one way of transferring risk. In this chapter we find that property and casualty insurance uses the principle of sharing risk. Where life insurance is easy to talk about because it is fairly uniform from state to state, property and casualty insurance is not.

As an example, look at **automobile insurance.** Some states require that automobile liability insurance be settled on a no-fault basis, while others rely on the justice system to settle disputed claims. Even those states that have no-fault insurance have different tort thresholds at which the legal system "kicks in." With such diversity comes much confusion. The potential losses incurred by a person can be catastrophic.

Homeowner's insurance is another guard against unexpected disasters that can cause catastrophic loss. In an instant, a fire could destroy the family home. Paying off the original mortgage and getting funds to build a new house could wipe out a family's savings.

It should be pointed out that **personal umbrella liability coverage** is available at relatively little additional cost. This type of policy gives additional protection beyond the basic coverage provided in homeowner and automobile insurance. For example, with a $1 million personal umbrella limit added to the $100,000 limit provided by Section II of a homeowner policy, a person injured at their home could conceivably collect up to $1.1 million.

Besides specifying excess limits of liability coverage, personal umbrella coverage will often provide broader protection than available in underlying contracts. Contracts may provide personal injury coverage and worldwide protection. Some policies even offer limited director's and officer's liability insurance for those people who serve on the board of nonprofit corporations such as churches and civic organizations. Premiums for up to $1 million coverage is less than $150 annually. Considering the low cost for this kind of coverage, it is a wise investment.

6 Homeowner's Insurance

Uses and Provisions

Homeowner's insurance is used to insure one's personal property and home against loss from various risks and perils. The policy is divided into two sections. Section I of the policy insures against property losses while Section II of the policy protects against loss from liability and medical expense payments to others, claim expenses, and damage to the property of others. As is true with automobile physical damage, a deductible applies to the property section of the homeowner's policy.

Section I **(property losses)** insures the property itself, including additions. Limited coverage is included for landscaping around the building (Coverage A). Other structures on the property such as a garage are included (Coverage B). Also, personal property named within the contract is covered (Coverage C). This coverage may have a low limit. Therefore, a rider for jewelry, furs, cameras, etc. should be added to provide adequate coverage. After losses incurred from a robbery, many people are shocked to find that their losses are not completely covered by insurance. Section I will also pay expenses incurred while the dwelling is uninhabitable due to loss from a covered peril (Coverage D).

Because homeowner's insurance comes in a variety of packages, it is important to understand how insurance companies package them. They like to divide coverage into two groups. The first is called **basic coverage** and the second is called **broad form coverage**.

Basic coverage include losses from fire and lightning, windstorm and hail, explosion, riot and civil commotion, vehicles, aircraft, smoke, vandalism and malicious mischief, glass breakage, and theft.

Broad form coverage includes the above plus falling objects, weight of ice, snow or sleet, collapse of a building, accidental discharge or overflow of water or steam, explosion of steam or hot water system, freezing of plumbing, heating or air conditioning systems, and damage from artifically generated electrical currents.

There are **nine classes of property excluded from all homeowners' policies.** They are articles separately described and specifically insured under homeowner's or other insurance policies. Further, animals, birds, and fish are excluded. Motorized land vehicles, aircraft, and their parts (except model or hobby aircraft), property of roomers, boarders, and other tenants not related to the insured are excluded too. (People who rent are expected to insure themselves with an HO-4 policy.) Other exclusions include property contained in an apartment regularly rented or held for rental to others by the insured, property rented or held for rental to others away from premises, books of account, drawings, paper records, and EDP software media containing business data, credit cards or fund transfer cards, except as provided under additional coverages.

Selection of which package to choose should be based on the type of property to be insured and the type of coverage to be provided. HO-1 (basic form), HO-2 (broad form), and HO-3 (special form) are the most common coverages used. There is a difference in approach by the insurance companies in issuing these policies. HO-1 and HO-2 offer named peril coverage, whereas the HO-3 provides all risk or open perils coverage. From the insured's point of view, HO-3 is a better deal; it provides coverage for all perils except those specifically listed in the contract. The HO-1 and HO-2 policies only insure those items specifically stated in the policy.

To demonstrate how the HO-3 policy may provide coverage in an unexpected situation, consider the following: You have in your living room expensive wall-to-wall carpeting. While cleaning, you spill caustic chemicals on the carpet. Under an HO-3 policy the insurance company will pay for the cost of repair or replacement of the carpet (less your deductible). Under the HO-1 or HO-2 policies, this would not be covered unless specifically stated.

There are times where the replacement value exceeds the market value of a house. This happens when a property was originally constructed of materials or by techniques that have become expensive to duplicate in today's market. Using a conventional homeowner's policy the cost of the premium could be prohibitive, so a HO-8 policy can be used for this purpose. The type of coverage specified is usually basic coverage.

For people who own condominiums, a HO-6 policy is used. This policy covers named perils on the unit's contents as well as additional coverages designed exclusively for condominiums.

Renters should purchase an HO-4 policy that covers the contents of their rental units. Aside from families who are renters, this is particularly useful when children go away to college and bring their stereos, computers, etc.

HO-5 policies are similar to HO-3 policies in that they cover all perils. In addition, they cover risks not usually covered by HO-3 policies such as flood and earthquake protection as well as damage from ground, water, etc. Because this covers virtually every risk up to the limits specified in the policy, HO-5 is the most expensive. Care should be used when purchasing a homeowner's policy to decide which one fits your particular needs.

The following chart summarizes the homeowner's coverages:

Homeowner's Coverages
Section I: Property

	Coverage A Dwelling	Coverage B Other Structures	Coverage C Personal Property	Coverage D Loss of Use
HO-1* HO-8*	Basic Basic $15,000 minimum	Basic Basic 10% of A	Basic Basic 50% of A	Basic Basic 10% of A
HO-2	Broad form $15,000 minimum	Broad form 10% of A	Broad form 50% of A	Broad form 20% of A
HO-3	All risk $20,000	All risk 10% of A	Broad form 50% of A	All risk 20% of A
HO-4	not covered (1)	not covered (1)	Broad form $6,000 min	Broad form 20% of C
HO-5	All risk $30,000 min	All risk 10% of A	All risk 50% of A	All risk 20% of A
HO-6	Not Covered (2)	Not Covered (2)	Broad form $6,000 min	Broad form 40% of C

*Ho-1 claims are settled on a replacement cost basis. HO-8 claims are settled on an actual cash value basis.
(1) HO-4 is a tenant's policy
(2) HO-6 is a condominium owner's policy

7 Personal Automobile Policy

An Overview

The personal automobile policy contains two main coverage sections. They are called **physical damage** and **liability.** In turn, the physical damage section has two parts. They are **collision** and **comprehensive.**

Collision provides coverage for the insured's automobile in the event that it collides with another object, or overturns. When considering the additional coverage to an automobile policy, the "book value" of the vehicle should be compared to the premium increase the premium represents. If the cost of the insurance is more than the expected amount recovered following a collision loss, such coverage would not be advisable. Sometimes the book value of an automobile is not always a true reflection of the car's true value. For example, an antique car may have a low "book value," but because of its "collector's value," it should be appraised and insured for more.

Comprehensive coverage, simply defined, is anything that can happen to a car except collision or an exception spelled out in the policy. Both collision and comprehensive use a deductible. In most states, unless a leasing company or lending institution requires them, they are optional coverages.

FINANCIAL RESPONSIBILITY LAWS

The basis for personal automobile insurance is the financial responsibility laws that all states have. They require drivers furnish evidence of financial responsibility after an accident. Not only the driver of a personally owned automobile, but the owner as well, must post security to guarantee payment of a judgment for an accident or bodily injury. This may be in the form of insurance, state minimum amount of cash, or bond. For most people insurance allows the most convenient way to do this.

A personal auto is defined as being owned by an individual or spouse living in the same household. The automobile must be for private use and not used as a livery or public conveyer.

PERSONAL AUTOMOBILE POLICY FORMAT

The personal automobile policy has six sections. You should be aware that the *first four sections may have their own agreements and exclusions.* The six sections are as follows:

    Part A - Liability coverage
    Part B - Medical payments
    Part C - Uninsured motorists
    Part D - Coverage for damage to your automobile
    Part E - Duties after an accident or loss
    Part F - General provisions

Liability coverage provides for bodily injury and property damage under a single insuring agreement. This eliminates the need for separate coverage for anyone operating the vehicle without the reasonable belief that he is entitled to do so. Therefore, you, your family, or anyone else to whom you give permission is covered while driving your automobile.

Other persons or organizations may be covered under this

section, but only with respect to legal responsibility for acts or omission of a person for whom coverage is afforded under this part. It applies only if the person or organization does not own or hire the automobile or trailer.

Coverage is for the vehicle shown in the declaration or any vehicle of which you acquire ownership during the policy period (providing you apply for insurance within thirty days). A pickup truck, van, or trailer is covered so long as it is not used for business or commercial purposes.

There are some limits to the liability section. The stipulations state that the limit per accident applies to *all* losses resulting out of a single accident. If necessary, the single limit will be applied as a split limit when required by law—subject to the condition that the insured's total limit of liability is not increased.

There are many exclusions under the liability section. Coverage is lost if the damage or bodily injury is intentional. Property owned or transported that becomes damaged is also excluded. Further, property that is damaged, rented to, used by, or in the care of the insured is excluded. Liability is not allowed if a person is being transported for hire. There is no coverage for any person operating an automobile while employed in the automobile business. The basic intent of this exclusion is to eliminate coverage for business use of commercial vehicles. (There are commercial policies available for this purpose.) Another exclusion removes coverage for any person who operates the vehicle without the reasonable belief that he is entitled to do so. Motorcycles or other self-propelling vehicles with under four wheels are excluded from coverage. Liability coverage is not allowed on vehicles owned by or furnished for regular use by the named insured, other than a covered vehicle (e.g., a company-owned car). Finally, there is a liability exclusion arising out of automobiles owned by or furnished for regular use by family members. This exclusion does not apply to the named insured or their spouse.

MEDICAL PAYMENTS

This section pays reasonable expenses incurred for necessary medical and funeral services because of bodily injury caused by an accident and sustained by a covered person. This provision will continue for up to three years.

There are some exclusions in the medical payments section too.

Payment will not be made for bodily injury under the following situations:

1. While occupying a vehicle of fewer than four wheels.
2. While occupying your covered automobile when it is being used to carry people for a fee. (This doesn't include a shared expense carpool.)
3. When the vehicle is used for residential purposes.
4. If worker's compensation benefits are required or available for bodily injury.
5. When an injury is sustained while occupying or when struck by any vehicle other than your covered vehicle.
6. Sustained while occupying a vehicle without a reasonable belief that person is entitled to do so.
7. Sustained while occupying a vehicle when it is being used in the business or occupation of a covered person. This exclusion does not apply to bodily injury sustained while occupying a private passenger vehicle, pickup or panel truck, van you own, or a trailer used in conjunction with the above.
8. If the bodily injury is caused by discharge of a nuclear weapon, war (declare or undeclared), civil war, insurrection or rebellion or revolution.
9. As a consequence of a nuclear reaction, radiation, or radiation contamination.

Coverage is limited to the persons covered, claims made, vehicles premiums shown in the declaration, and the vehicles involved in the accident. If other insurance is available, each company will pay its proportional share.

UNINSURED MOTORIST

There is a section in the personal automobile policy that pays the injured insured an amount that could have been collected from the insurer of an uninsured driver had the person had coverage. In this situation, the insured and his family members are covered. Also, all other occupants of the car are covered. Again the old rules apply: prohibition of using the vehicle for commercial purposes and the occupants must have the consent of the owner to be in the car. *If the insured settles with the negligent party without the insurer's consent, no coverage will be allowed.*

Underinsured Motorist

This section provides coverage when the negligent party has insurance, but it is insufficient to cover the damage to the insured. This is usually added as a rider to the policy.

This part of the policy covers damage to your car aside from collision (comprehensive) protection. Exclusions under this section include breakage of glass, tape recorders, tapes, records, and other media designed for use with sound reproducing equipment. Camper bodies and trailers not listed in the declarations are not covered. Transmitting and receiving equipment (e.g., CB and amateur radio equipment, cellular telephones) are not covered. Many features of customized vans are similarly excluded.

It should be noted that the insurance company may seek an appraisal for damaged property. If you disagree, you may get your own appraiser. If they should disagree, an umpire agreed upon by the appraisers makes the final decision. Each party shares the cost of the appraisal dispute equally.

Duties of the Insured

When an accident occurs, the insured must notify the insurance company promptly. Further, they must cooperate with the insurer by providing all legal documents, medical records, and results of physical examinations. Also, proof of the loss is required.

Automobile Insurance Checklist

	Auto 1	Auto 2	Auto 3
Liability ($)			
Uninsured motorist			
Underinsured motorist			
Medical payments			
Personal injury protection			
Collision			
Deductible			
Annual premium			
Riders			
Towing and labor			
Luggage and apparel			
Rental reimbursement			

8 Liability Insurance

There are several different forms of liability insurance, including personal and commercial forms. Many of the personal forms are part of other policies, for example, homeowners and automobile policies. Commercial policies have their own particular features.

The term "professional liability" refers to liability arising from a failure to use due care and the degree of skill expected by a person in a particular profession. For physicians, dentists, and attornies, when bodily injury is involved, it is called "malpractice insurance." For people in the insurance or financial planning industries and other professions, it is called "errors and omission insurance."

For physicians and dentists, the need for malpractice insurance is obvious. Aside from liability protection against bodily injury, protection is given against error in judgment, battery, assault, actions taken without patient's consent, libel and slander in connection with breach of professional confidence, imprisonment or wrongful detention, and invasion of privacy. Errors and omissions insurance protects the financial services person against errors of judgment and failure to inform his/

her client about various risks. Often, other small business owners must carry product and premises liability as well.

Some unique features of these policies deserve comment. Coverage is not limited to property damage or bodily injury; losses from mental anguish and intentional acts are also covered.

Until recently, these policies were written as **occurrence policies.** These protected the business owner if the injury or wrong took place while the policy was in force. So even if the loss was discovered twenty years later, the insured was covered. This resulted in a "long tail" on losses and made it difficult for insurance companies to price these policies.

Today most insurance companies issue **claims made** policies. With this type of policy, the claim must be made during the time the policy is in force. Because of this, if an insured retires from practice before normal retirement age, it is frequently necessary to prepay two or three years of premium to maintain coverage until the local statutes of limitation expire.

Under the old style of policy the insurance company had to get permission from the business owner to settle a claim. This was to protect the reputation of the business. Payment of the claim by an insurance company might have been considered an admission of guilt. The way that the newer policies are written, consent of the insured is not necessary for the insurance company to make an out-of-court settlement.

In the section about homeowner's insurance, use of an **umbrella** policy was discussed. The same principles apply to professional and business liability policies as well. The cost for the increased coverage above the basic policy provisions is small compared to the larger and broader coverage provided.

9 Health Insurance

❦

AN OVERVIEW

Health insurance provides coverage against medical expense and disability income risk exposures. Without adequate coverage, a serious illness, accident, or disability could be catastrophic for a family. Today health insurance comes in many forms. For paying physicians and hospital bills there is basic coverage, major medical, and comprehensive coverages. A recent wrinkle has been the introduction of health maintenance organizations (HMO's) and preferred provider organizations (PPO's). These attempt to provide limited comprehensive coverage through cost containment procedures.

Disability insurance is often overlooked, though, until one reaches a certain age, when the odds of becoming disabled increase. Along with disability insurance, overhead expense should be strongly considered by most healthcare professionals. After all, who is going to pay the rent and office salaries and taxes if you are not working.

With our rapidly growing and aging population, more and more people are going to be spending part of their lives in nursing homes. Considering that this costs $3,000–$6,000 per month, a long-term care policy should be considered. This expense can rapidly deplete a family's lifetime savings. The results could leave the healthy spouse destitute.

10 Disability Income Insurance

Disability income insurance is intended to provide periodic payments to the insured when they are unable to work due to illness or accident. Though it may be added as a rider to a health insurance policy, it is usually purchased as a separate policy. *The key to collecting on this type of policy is the definition of disability.*

The strict definition of disability is **"any occupation."** To be considered disabled, the insured must not be able to perform any and every duty of any gainful occupation.

Social Security carries this even further. To be reimbursed by Social Security a person must be "totally disabled" for at least five months before they can even apply. Further, there must be a probability that the disability will last for at least twelve months. The applicant must have been eligible for Social Security for seven of the last thirteen quarters. This makes collecting for disability from Social Security very difficult.

The liberal definition of disability is **"own occupation."** To collect under this definition, the insured must not be able to do any duties of his/her profession. This is the preferred definition. **Be sure that you understand which definition your policy is using.**

Many policies issued today use a **"split definition."** Split definitions use the "own occupation" for a period of time (e.g., two years), then revert to "any occupation" after that.

There are some important features to clarify regarding disability policies. Obviously, the definition of disability is the first consideration. The policy should have guaranteed premium rates and not be cancellable up to age sixty-five. A waiver of premium clause is desirable if the insured is disabled for more than ninety days. Some policies offer cost-of-living adjustments. Others offer the opportunity to purchase additional disability coverage at standard rates regardless of medical insurability. Another desirable feature is a recurrent disability clause. This clause eliminates the waiting period if a person returns to work for six months and then becomes disabled from the same cause.

Recovery benefits should be checked to be certain that it is possible to collect some benefit if an individual should return to work part-time. Residual disability benefits will pay the difference between the reduced salary and the amount received from total disability benefits. This should continue as long as the insured can prove that he has at least 20 percent to 25 percent loss of income.

Besides looking at the policy's benefits, there are other things to consider. For example, while many policies pay up to 60 percent to 65 percent of income, others may pay as low as 40 percent. It is unlikely that you will find a policy that reimburses for your entire income. In reality it doesn't matter. One reason is that while disability income premiums are not deductible for solo proprietors or partnerships as a business expense, the disability income is not taxable. So it is a wash. A sick or disabled person may also have fewer expenses.

Another consideration is the cost of coverage. By using a longer waiting period or having separate waiting periods for accident and sickness, premiums can be kept reasonable. You should be aware that many policies reduce their payment when Social Security begins.

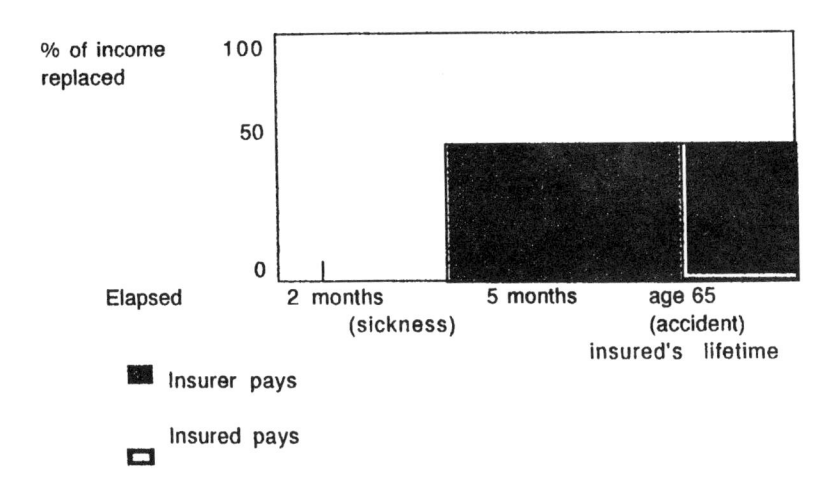

```
% of income      100
replaced
                  50

                   0
     Elapsed       2 months        5 months         age 65
                   (sickness)                       (accident)
                                                    insured's  lifetime
        ■  Insurer pays

        □  Insured pays
```

In this table, there is a two-month waiting (probation) period before the policy goes into effect. Since the insured decided on a ninety-day waiting period, it will be five months before the policy becomes effective. At that time the insured will begin to collect 50 percent of his previous monthly income.

A debilitating accident or illness can occur suddenly and without warning. Due to the inability to foresee such a possibility, most people would be wise to anticipate anything and protect themselves from severe financial loss. Yet, few people do.

OVERHEAD EXPENSE POLICIES

Overhead expense policies are similar to disability policies. Instead of covering the insured's personal expenses, they cover office and business expenses incurred during normal business operations. Examples of this might be rent, salaries, taxes, and supplies. This type of policy is especially useful for small businesses and professionals.

One important consideration to check is that the policy contains provisions for payment during *both* full and partial disabilities. Another noteworthy feature is that office overhead expense policies are frequently deductible as a business expense, whereas personal disability policies are not. On the flip side, the income from a disability policy is not taxable income, while the income from an office overhead expense policy is.

MEDICAL EXPENSE POLICIES

Medical expense policies are divided into four categories. They are **basic or regular coverage, major medical, comprehensive,** and **normal health maintenance organizations.**

Basic medical or **regular coverage** pays for surgical and hospital expenses up to a specified amount. It may also pay a limited portion of physician's fees for non-surgical expense. Basic medical coverage is often inadequate to pay for total medical expenses.

Major medical expense policies pay for medical care costs in and out of the hospital. They have higher limits than basic coverage. Premiums are determined by the deductible, the coinsurance percentage, and the break point. (This is the point where the insurer pays 100 percent of expense up to specific limits.) There are relatively few exclusions.

Comprehensive medical policies combine basic and major medical into a single policy. They usually have higher limits than major medical policies by themselves.

In recent years **health maintenance organizations** have sprung up. They provide comprehensive health care for a pre-negotiated lump sum or periodic payment. The subscriber must use their providers unless they are out of town or the necessary specialist does not belong to the organization. Often the provider is paid a specific sum per month for each person or family assigned to his office. This is regardless of the patient's problem. So some financial risk is transferred to the provider. In theory, some of this is offset by the healthy people who sign up for the plan but don't use it. Seldom does it work the way it is supposed to for the provider, but the members get most types of care.

MEDICARE

A modification of the major medical policy is the medigap policy. In 1965, the Medicare program was enacted. It was supposed to reduce the need for healthcare policies for people over sixty-five. The Medicare program is subject to deductibles and co-insurance provisions that change from year to year. To fill the "gap" in protection, commercial insurers and the Blue Cross and Blue Shield organizations have developed special policies to pay the difference between what Medicare pays and the actual cost of medical care.

Unfortunately, abuses have developed in this area. Some contracts sold as supplements are overpriced and offer inadequate coverage. The following outline describes the benefits of Medicare (Part A) and Medicare (Part B). The latter is the part of Medicare that requires supplemental coverage.

MEDICARE (Part A, 1995)

1.1 Hospitalization
    2.1 Semiprivate room and board, general nursing and miscellaneous hospital services and supplies (Medicare payments based on benefit periods)
        3.1 Benefit
            4.1 First 60 days
                5.1 Medicare pays all but $652
                5.2 You pay $716
            4.2 61st to 90th days
                5.2 Medicare pays all but $179 / day
                5.2 You pay $179 / day
            4.3 91st to 150th days (This 60-day reserve may be used only once in a lifetime)
                5.1 Medicare pays all but $358 / day
                5.2 You pay $358 / day
            4.4 Beyond 150 days
                5.1 Medicare pays nothing
                5.2 You pay everything
1.2 Skilled Nursing Facility Care (You must have been in a hospital for at least 3 days and enter a Medicare-approved facility generally within 30 days after hospital discharge)
2.1 First 20 days
        3.1 Medicare pays 100% of approved amount
        3.2 You pay nothing
    2.2 Additional 80 days
        3.1 Medicare all but $89.50 / day
        3.2 You pay $89.50 / day
    2.3 Beyond 80 days

3.1 Medicare pays nothing
   3.2 You pay all costs
1.3 Home Healthcare (Medically necessary skilled care)
   2.1 Part-time or intermittent care for as long as you meet Medicare conditions
      3.1 Medicare pays 100% of approved amount; 80% of approved amount for durable medical equipment
      3.2 You pay nothing for services; 20% for durable medical equipment
1.4 Hospice Care
   2.1 As long as doctor certifies need
      3.1 Medicare pays all but limited costs for outpatient drugs and inpatient respite care
      3.2 You pay limited cost for outpatient drugs and inpatient respite care
1.5 Blood
   2.1 Medicare pays for all but the first three pints
   2.2 You pay for the first three pints

Note: There is no premium for most beneficiaries. Those not elgible may purchase it for a premium of $192 per month. Neither Medicare (Part A) nor private Medigap policies pay for most nursing home care.

MEDICARE (Part B, 1995)
1.1 Medical Expenses
   2.1 Doctors' services, inpatient and outpatient medical and surgical services and supplies, physical and speech therapy, ambulance, diagnostic tests, and more
      3.1 Medicare pays for medical services in or out of the hospital (80% of approved amount after $100 deductible)
      3.2 You pay $100 deductible/year plus 20% of approved amount and limited charges above approved amount. (Physicians who do not accept assignment of Medicare claims are limited by law as to the amount they can charge a Medicare beneficiary for covered services. In 1992, the charge cannot be more than 120% of the Medicare fee schedule for physicians who do not participate in Medicare.)
1.2 Clinical Laboratory Services
   2.1 Medicare (Part B) pays for 100% of the approved amount
   2.2 You pay nothing
1.3 Home Health Care

2.1 Part-time or intermittent skilled care for as long as you meet conditions for benefits
   3.1 Medicare pays 100% of approved amount; 80% of approved amount for durable medical equipment
   3.2 You pay 20% of approved amount for durable medical equipment
1.4 Outpatient Hospital Treatment
   2.1 If medically necessary, Medicare (Part B) will pay for 80% of approved amount (after the $100 deductible)
   2.2 You pay $100 deductible, plus 20% of billed charges
1.5 Blood
   2.1 Medicare (Part B) will pay for 80% of approved amount after the $100 deductible (starting with the fourth pint)
   2.2 You pay for the first three pints, plus 20% of the approved amount for additional pints (after the $100 deductible)

Note: Monthly premiums (1995) are $46.10. If you enroll late, the premium may be higher.

11 Long-Term care Policies

Long-term care policies come in many variations. Since these types of policies are relatively new, people do not always understand what they are buying. They are supposed to pay for the cost of nursing home care and, under certain conditions, care at home during rehabilitation from accidents or chronic illness. Unfortunately, some policies have many restrictions.

Before discussing the various policy features, the definition of the various kinds of care available should be understood.

The first and least expensive form of care available is called **respite care.** It provides relief to the overburdened homecare provider for periods ranging from one hour to several days. In-home respite care is reimbursed by Medicare Part A when furnished by a hospice care provider. In these cases the recipient is expected to die within six months. Although this is the least expensive form of care, most insurance companies do *not* pay for this care.

In-home care (personal nursing care) is another form of coverage available. This care may range from unskilled to skilled (e.g., a housekeeper or registered nurse). The care provider may be independent or freelance. He/she may be hired by the family or be an employee of a corporation paid by the family. Most policies will only reimburse for skilled care. Only long-term comprehensive policies will pay for housekeeping, homemaker, and custodial care.

Another form of coverage is **adult foster care.** In this situation, the family member actually leaves home and resides where the care is delivered. Frequently, these are residential homes that have been converted for adult foster use. These facilities are reluctant to accept individuals with disruptive or potentially dangerous behavior problems. If the patient has medical problems requiring sophisticated medical care, he may be rejected. Specific skilled care is only provided by outside sources on a need basis.

Familiar to most people is **nursing home care.** Even in this setting reimbursement may be restricted by policy provisions. Some policies require that the patient be hospitalized before nursing home care will be paid. Others will only pay for skilled nursing home care. It is important to understand that there are different levels of nursing home care.

The first level of nursing home care is **custodial care.** It provides care to individuals not able to receive in-home care or adult foster care, but do not have complicated medical problems. Medicare, private major medical, and *Medicare* supplement policies do *not* pay for custodial nursing home care. *Medicaid* will reimburse for this coverage.

Intermediate care requires "total care" twenty-four hours per day. Though the patient may have a few help skills, they may have complicated medical problems or may not be able to perform many activities of daily living. This must be supervised by a registered nurse.

The highest level of nursing home care is **skilled nursing care.** At this level the individual has almost no self-help skills and has complicated medical management needs, requiring the skills of a registered nurse (total care). This care is the most expensive. Medicare and private major medical insurance reimburses for up to 100 days of skilled nursing home care. *Many policies require that the patient be hospitalized for three days within thirty days admission to a nursing home.* Because of this foolishness, if care is required outside the definitions of skilled care, no reimbursement may be possible. Policies with this provision should be avoided.

There are many other features to be reviewed. The kind of underwriting at the time the policy is written should be checked. Group underwriting makes it easier for an individual with minor health problems to receive some benefits, though they may be limited. A healthy person taking out a long-term care policy might be able to obtain more liberal allowances.

Obviously, the policy should be renewable for life. There should not be any individual premium increases unless reflected in the class as a whole. Nor should there be premium increases due to increased age.

As alluded to previously, the forms of reimbursed care should be carefully checked. Facility care and care provider definitions should be understood. Further, the level of care sequence should not discriminate initial care levels for reimbursement.

Medically necessary care definitions should be reviewed. For example, some policies will not pay reimbursement for mental illness, dementia and Alzheimer's disease. Others will not pay for pre-existing conditions. Some require shorter waiting periods. (When looking at the out-of-pocket costs for nursing home care, shorter waiting periods may be false economy.)

Another feature to look for is a waiver of premium if the insured remains in a period of continuous covered care for a specified number of days. Make sure you have an adequate daily rate, and that care costs are automatically adjusted for inflation. Many policies have a coordination of benefits. Finally, the policy payments should be for a minimum of three or four years duration.

Checklist for Long-Term Care

Daily rate	_____
Coordination of benefits	_____
Inflation protection	_____

Duration of policy _____
Waiver of premium
  for continued disability _____
Policy renewable for life _____
Type of underwriting _____
Skill levels covered:
  In-home care _____
  Adult foster care _____
  Custodial care _____
  Intermediate care _____
  Skilled care _____
Policy restrictions:
  Hospital admission
    prior to payment _____
  Mental illness _____
  Dementia & Alzheimer's _____
Waiting period _____

References

Baldwin, Benjamin, G., CFP, ChFC, CLU; "New Frontier in Health Insurance: Medical, Disability, and Long Term Care," National Conference, Denver, Colorado, 1991.

Bevington, Virginia A., CFP, CLU; "Insurance Products: Cash Value Life Insurance and Annuities," National Conference, Denver, Colorado, 1991.

Cady, Donald F., JD, LLM, LLU, "Estate Planning and Survivorship Life Insurance Policy," National Conference, Denver, Colorado, 1991.

Miterko, Peter M., Esq., "Incentive and Deferred Compensation for the Corporate Executive," National Conference, Denver, Colorado, 1991.

Saenger, Bruce W., "Structuring Property/Casualty Insurance Programs," *Personal Financial Planning*, July–August, 1992, Warren, Gorham, Lamont, p.p 34–40.

Seal, Gregory P., CFP, "Long Term Health Insurance," National Conference, Denver, Colorado, 1990.

Social Security Administration, Medicare Benefits, 1992.

Vaughan, Emmett J., Fundamentals of Risk and Insurance, 4th edition, 1986, John Wiley and Sons, New York, N.Y.

12 Savings

As suggested in Chapter 2, "Getting Out of Debt," savings constitutes the foundation of any wealth management program. Until now we have been concerned with creating an estate and protecting it. Now we begin the "fun" part of wealth management–accumulation. You would be amazed at the amount of satisfaction and stress release that comes with the realization that you are slowly, but surely, getting richer.

What are some reasons to save money? The first and foremost is to have a reserve fund to tide you over in case of emergency. Most planners recommend three to four months income for this purpose. As a side issue, the three months reserve allows you to self-insure for disability, health and accident insurance. By buying a policy with a larger deductible, you pay a significantly lower premium. Other uses for savings are children's college education, retirement planning, and security for loans. (Remember, banks don't lend money to people who have nothing.)

There are many kinds of savings. The most common is the **passbook savings account.** Essentially, you lend the bank your money at a given rate. They pay you interest. The interest is compounded quarterly or daily and credited to your account on a quarterly basis. Beware that 5 percent interest compounded daily is a higher annual rate than 5 percent compounded quarterly or annually. Some passbook accounts do not compound the interest until the last day of the quarter. If you were to have a large balance during the quarter and take it out two days before the end of the quarter, you could conceivably receive no interest on your savings.

Another type of savings offered by banking institutions are **certificates of deposit or CDs.** Unlike passbook accounts where a person can withdraw his money on demand, money placed in CDs must remain there until they mature. Due to this restriction, banks must pay a higher rate of interest than on passbook savings. Some banks allow people to withdraw accrued interest every six months without penalty. If the principal is withdrawn early, there is a six month penalty.

Many people who lived through the Great Depression will only buy certificates of deposit and passbook savings because they are "insured" by the U. S. government up to $100,000. This is ironic because the actual insurance in the federal agency accounts that insure them is small. This explains why Congress had to allocate funds for the savings and loan bailout. The same thing could happen with commercial banks as well.

Another risk not noticed by many people with passbook savings and certificates of deposit is that they pay a low rate of interest relative to inflation. For example, let us say that a 5 percent inflation rate exists. The bank pays 5 percent interest on passbook savings. The depositor pays taxes on the interest. After federal and local taxes are paid, he is left with 3 percent on his money. It does not keep up with inflation in purchasing power. In later years it will cost more dollars to buy the same items than it does today.

Money market funds are another popular form of savings. They are offered by mutual fund companies. Though they are *not* insured by any federal agency, most are considered safe. This is because they invest primarily in short-term U.S. Government securities. The rates of return are slightly higher than bank savings accounts. Still, you should read the prospectuses to find out how they invest your money.

Money market shares are valued at $1 par value, so shares may be redeemed on demand. Some money market funds have check-writing privileges. Often there is a $500 minimum.

In competition with money market funds, many banks offer **interest bearing checking accounts.** They offer interest on the average daily balance in the account. This is credited at the cut-off date each month. There are no restrictions to the minimum amount for which a check can be written. Often, a line of credit (called ready reserve) can be established with this to provide an automatic loan if needed.

An easy way to save money is with **EE savings bonds.** They are issued by the United States government and backed by the full faith and credit of the United States. They can be purchased at any commercial bank with no commission or fees. Frequently, people arrange to purchase these bonds through a payroll deduction plan. The bonds are bought at one half their face value. When they mature in twelve years, the investor gets back at least the face value of the bond. They are available in denominations of $25 to $10,000.

EE savings bonds have several advantages over passbook accounts and CDs. First, after two months they are available on demand with accrued interest. Second, the interest on EE bonds is tax deferred until the bond is "cashed." Even then, if the proceeds are used to help to pay the tuition and books of post–high school education, the interest may be exempt from taxes. (If the family's joint annual income is over $60,000, the tax benefit gradually reduces as it approaches $90,000.)

Interest on EE bonds is a minimum of 4 percent if the bonds are held for five years. If cashed in before five years, the interest is determined by the short-term treasury rate from the time the bond was purchased. For bonds held over five years, the interest rate is tied to 85 percent of the rate for five-year treasury notes. As this is adjusted every May and November, so there is some inflation protection.

HH bonds are also issued by the United States government. Like the EE bonds, they are backed by the United States government. They are available in denominations of $500 multiples. They are purchased at face value and mature in ten years. HH bonds can only be purchased from the proceeds of the redemption of EE bonds. Again, the interest is tax-deferred. Purchasing HH bonds is still another way of deferring payment on the accrued interest of EE bonds. They may be redeemed at any time.

Credit unions operate in much the same way as banks. Usually they are chartered by the state. They operate for the benefit of a specific group. The interest rates they pay are generally a little higher than banks pay on savings accounts. The rates charged members for loans and other services are usually lower. Safety depends on the investments made by its investment group.

Though not thought of by many people, **cash value life insurance policies** are a form of savings. The ability of people to "borrow" out a large percentage of the cash value in time of emergency makes them a unique form of savings. This has been discussed in more detail in the chapter on life insurance.

Some important considerations when choosing a savings vehicle are insured versus non-insured accounts, what is left after taxes, and the future value of the account in terms of purchasing power. These have been previously discussed.

13 Retirement Planning

Cost of Retirement

If you were to ask a financial planner when you should begin planning for retirement, he would probably answer: the day that you began to work. Few people do. In fact most people don't even begin to think seriously about retiring until their children are through school. Usually, this is not until their mid-fifties.

Yet early retirement planning has much merit. As an example let's look at two people.

Sally opens an IRA account on her nineteenth birthday and makes nine $2,000 contributions (ending on her twenty-seventh birthday), then stops. David decides to open an IRA account on his twenty-seventh birthday and makes thirty-nine $2,000 contributions through his sixty-fifth birthday. If each earns 10 percent return per year (income plus growth), which will have the larger IRA at age sixty-five?

The answer may surprise you. Sally will have $1,015,864. David will have only $802,889. Though Sally made only nine contributions and David will have made thirty-nine, Sally will have had eight extra years of compounding.

Whether a person is just beginning his career or counting the number of days until retirement, this chapter presents many thoughtful suggestions for your retirement. By preparing a retirement budget now and preparing for it in advance, some quantifying goals can be defined and may provide future peace of mind. Certain assumptions about inflation, taxes, the growth of your money, and your longevity must be made. Working through the numbers should give you a reasonable idea as to how much should be saved annually.

The first step is to figure out the annual income you will need for a comfortable retirement. The good news is that you will not need to replace 100 percent of your income. Most financial planners believe that a person can maintain the same standard of living at 70–80 percent of their preretirement income. This is because housing costs, transportation, and clothing costs will be significantly lower. On the other hand, medical costs and entertainment costs usually increase. For many people, Social Security provides an average of 20 percent of their preretirement income. Pensions often provide 40–60 percent of preretirement income. This means that the balance must be made up through working or other sources. People frequently wonder how long it takes to accumulate a certain amount of money. Of course, this depends on the rate of return one gets on his investments. For example, if someone wanted to have one million dollars in thirty years, he would have to set aside $6,700 into a tax-deferred account paying 9 percent. If the same amount is needed in ten years, payments of $60,000 per year would have to be made. (To figure out how much you must save each year, see the Retirement Planning Worksheet at the end of this chapter.)

Another question often asked is how long will my money last? Many individuals live an austere retirement on the interest from their investments only because they are afraid of outliving their money. The answer, of course, depends on what rate of return an individual receives on his investments plus the amount he will withdraw each year. For example, a fund earning 8 percent will last twenty years if you withdraw 10 percent each year. The same fund would last twenty-eight years if one would draw only 9 percent per year. The extra 1 or 2 percent may not seem like a lot, but it can make the difference between having a comfortable retirement or not. Also, it helps to know one's life expectancy, so consult the Projected Life Expectancy chart below.

A useful rule used in financial planning is the "rule of 72." It takes seventy-two years for a sum of money to double, earning a 1 percent rate of return annually. The way it works is to divide the rate of interest one receives on an investment into 72. The results are the number of years it takes to double one's money. For example, let us say that one's pension plan currently has $500,000. This may be about half of what will be needed for retirement. Let us pretend the portfolio is receiving an 8 percent rate of return. To find out how long it will take for this to double, we divide 8 percent into 72 and we get 9 years. The "rule of 72" also works in reverse. So one can divide the number of years into 72 to find the rate of return necessary to receive on investments. This is a quick way to decide whether investment goals are being met.

It is obvious that to have a comfortable retirement, planning should begin early. Once a retirement plan has been developed, it should be implemented and reviewed periodically to make sure it still reflects one's goal.

Retirement Planning Worksheet

This worksheet will help decide how much you need to put away today to enjoy the standard of living you want tomorrow. Figures are in current before tax dollars, so allow enough to pay for your taxes and keep up with inflation.

1. Projected annual income needed — $_____
2. Estimated retirement income from various sources (Social Security, pensions, etc.) — -_____
3. Annual retirement income shortfall — =_____
4. Assumed rate of return on investments (e.g., If you assume an 8 percent rate of return, divide by .08) — #3 / #4
5. Gross amount needed to provide annual retirement shortfall — =_____
6. Current savings — _____

7. Growth factor   x_____
8. Future value of savings   =_____
9. Additional savings needed
   (line 5 minus line 8)   _____
10. Savings factor   x_____
11. Annual savings goal   =_____

Years to retirement	5	10	15	20	25	30
Growth factor*	1.47	2.16	3.17	4.66	6.85	10.06
Savings factor**	.170	.069	.033	.019	.013	.008

*The growth factor shows how much $1 invested at 8 percent will be worth in various numbers of years.

**The savings factor shows the amount that must be deposited, earning 8 percent annually, to net $1 after a given period.

Projected Life Expectancy

Current Age

Age	Men	Current Life Expectancy Women
25	76.2	83.1
45	77.3	82.9
65	80.6	84.9
85	90.5	91.9

Source: Social Security Administration

Another helpful aid is the table below. It states the amount that must be saved each month, at different ages and interest rates, to achieve $100,000 by age sixty-five.

Monthly Payments to Achieve $100,000 by Age 65

Age	5%	6%	7%	8%	9%	10%
25	65	50	38	29	21	16
35	118	99	82	67	55	44
45	255	216	192	170	150	132
55	644	610	578	547	517	488
65	—	—	—	—	—	—

14 Sources of Retirement Income

After going through the exercise in the previous chapter, it should be obvious that most people do not adequately plan for retirement. So what are some sources of retirement income?

Obviously, if you don't have enough investment income you can continue to work full or part-time. Since statistics from various sources over the years show that only 20 percent of the people are financially secure at retirement, this is one option.

Another source of retirement income comes from the United States Government. Usually, this is from three sources. They are **Social Security, Civil Service, and other pension plans, e. g. the military.**

Originally, the Social Security Act of 1935 established a federally operated system for distributing old age benefits to commerce and industry workers sixty-five and older. Over the years the act has been amended to provide additional benefits. These include benefits for disability and death benefits.

According to the Social Security Administration, nine out

of ten workers in the United States are earning protection credit under Social Security. Approximately one out of six people receive a monthly Social Security check. More than twenty-four million people over sixty-five have health insurance under Medicare. Another three million disabled people under sixty-five receive Medicare assistance.

The Social Security trust fund receives its funding from a combination of payroll deductions from the employee's paycheck, with matching contributions from one's employer. In 1993, the contribution was 7.65 percent of salary each for the employer and employee and up to a maximum of $57,600. This has been adjusted periodically. Beginning in 1994, an additional 2.9 percent (1.45 percent each for employers and employees) will apply without limit as a Medicare tax.

To be eligible, you must earn credits for working. The number of credits is dependent on your numbers of credits worked and your age. Earnings of $590 merit one quarter of credit. A maximum of 4 credits per year can be earned.

So how much are you going to receive from Social Security when you retire? The easiest way to find out is to call or write the Social Security office and ask for a request for benefits form. (The toll free number is 1-800-772-1213.) It is a short form. After you send it in, you will receive a printout of all your contributions. Further, it tells how much you will receive in terms of today's dollars when you reach sixty-two, sixty-five, and seventy. Disability payments, death benefits, and family survivor benefits are listed.

Social Security benefits are based on earnings averaged over most of a worker's lifetime. This is different from many other pension plans that are based on a relatively small number of years of earnings. Thirty-five years of earnings are used to figure the average monthly earnings. This is called the **primary insured amount (PIA).** If you haven't worked for that number of years when you reach normal retirement, they will add in years of zero earnings to make up the difference.

A new formula is set each year for people reaching age sixty-two. The percentages remain the same, but the dollar amounts change. This is because Social Security payments are adjusted for inflation on an annual basis. If you should decide to retire at age sixty-two, your benefits will be reduced by 5/9 of 1 percent for each month you receive benefits before age sixty-five.

One interesting aspect of Social Security that has potential is spousal benefits. A spouse who did not work, worked very little, or "helped out" in a family business for no pay, may, at the age sixty-five, apply to Social Security to receive up to one-half the amount that the major wage earner receives. This is instead of what they would receive based on their contributions.

Widow(er)s and divorced people may also be entitled to Social Security benefits based on their spouse's contributions under certain circumstances. These should not be overlooked as sources of income.

Beginning in 1994, depending on income levels, up to 85 percent of Social Security benefits may be taxed. This may occur when provisional income levels (modified adjusted gross income plus one-half Social Security benefits) rise above $34,000 for an unmarried filer and $44,000 on a joint return. The formula for computing this is complex and should be done by an accountant.

It should be noted that it is possible to lose Social Security benefits if you continue to work after retiring. In 1994, if you are 65–69 years old and earned over $11,160, your Social Security benefit would be reduced by $1 for every $3 that you earned over that amount. If you were over sixty-two but under sixty-five and earned more than $7,800, your benefit would be reduced $1 for every $2 earned over that amount. You will notice that the key is "earned" income. Most investment income is exempt. These maximums have been adjusted each year to reflect cost of living adjustments. Currently there is a bill in Congress to eliminate these restrictions. Only time will tell if they are enacted.

Another source of government benefits are **Civil Service pensions.** The basis for this is the Civil Service Act of 1920. This too had been amended over the years to reflect changes in the economy. It encompasses all employees of the federal government, federally controlled corporations, and employees of the District of Columbia if employed by December 31, 1983.

The Vice President, members of Congress and their staffs are included in the program only if they chose to join by December 31, 1983.

Federal employees and employee groups excluded from Civil Service include the President of the United States, and other employees covered by their own programs, such as the Foreign Service, the District of Columbia Teachers Association, and the Tennessee Valley Authority Retirement System.

The 1983 Social Security Amendment impacted on Civil Service–mandated Social Security coverage for all federal employees hired on or after January 1, 1984. This included those with previous periods of federal service if the break in service lasted at least 365 days. Employees who were previously excluded from Civil Service coverage and those who had elected not to be covered in the Civil Service Program now have mandatory Social Security coverage.

Like Social Security, the Civil Service Retirement Act provides benefits in three areas: retirement, disability, and survivor income. Since we are discussing retirement, our discussion will be confined to this area.

Retirement benefits are paid in four categories: full immediate retirement annuity, reduced immediate retirement annuity, deferred retirement annuity, and joint and survivorship retirement annuity.

Civil Service pensions are funded by employee contributions that are matched by the federal government. Employee contributions are based on a percentage of basic salary. This excludes any bonuses, allowances, overtime, and military pay.

Each of the annuities requires the same amount of credited service for eligibility. Credit is counted for both civilian and military service. One or five years of covered civilian employment in the two years before separation from covered employment are included.

Two exceptions to receiving full credit toward eligibility are as follows:

1) Any period of covered employment in which the employee receives a refund of contributions will not be considered credited service unless the employee repays the amount with interest.

2) Any period in which an employee is granted a leave of absence without pay is credited in full up to six months of service per calendar year.

As indicated above, both civilian and military time count toward Civil Service. In addition to total years of service, an average basic salary must be determined. This average annual salary is based upon the employee's highest basic salary earnings over a consecutive three-year period. This period need not be in calendar years. Like Social Security, Civil Service annuities receive cost of living adjustments.

Civil service benefits are not integrated with other benefit plans. Therefore, a retiree can receive both Social Security and Civil Service benefits concurrently.

The federal tax status of Civil Service annuities is similar to commercial annuities. In general, employee contributions are not deductible, and retirement annuities are taxable.

There are many rules that govern the computation and eligibility of civil service annuities. It is not my intention that you know all the details of how to do this. What is important is that you have a general understanding about the benefits available.

Members of the **uniformed services** are entitled to government pensions as well. The uniformed services consist of individuals who serve in the regular military, Coast Guard, Geodetic Survey, and U.S. Public Health Service. Reserve members of these branches of the service and the National Guard are included. Time spent as cadets of the service academies counts toward retirement.

Eligibility for retirement benefits is based upon credited years of service and base pay of the highest rank held during service. There is an optional reduction in benefit should there be an annuity provision for an eligible survivor.

Active duty members must have a minimum of twenty years service to be eligible for minimum pension (50 percent of base pay). For each year between twenty and thirty, retirement pay increases by 2.5 persent per year to a maximum of 75 percent of base pay.

Reserve members must be at least sixty years old, have completed a minimum of twenty years of federal service, be ineligible for any other armed forces retirement pay or benefit, and have served the last eight years of qualifying service in a reserve unit. A point system for various service-related activities determines the number of years of credit. Fifty points count as one year of satisfactory service.

Uniform services retirement benefits are not integrated with Social Security. Therefore, it is possible for a retired service person to receive all service-connected retirement benefits and Social Security benefits. Uniformed Service benefits are federally taxable income.

Previously, it was mentioned that an optional survivor benefit plan is available. The survivor benefit annuity to a surviving spouse of a retired service member will be reduced dollar-for-dollar up to 50 percent for any Social Security benefit.

Because individual factors can affect the survivor benefit offset calculations, uniformed personnel should contact their local service benefit office for detailed descriptions of their situations.

15 Pension Plans

In general, most pension plans in the private sector are tax favored. They allow individuals and companies to put aside dollars on a tax-deferred basis during the employee's working years. When the employee retires, he is paid out as retirement income. Distributions may also be paid out in cases of death or disability.

There are many types of pension plans. Examples include Individual Retirement Accounts (IRAs), Simplified Employee Pensions (SEPs), and corporate pension and profitsharing plans. Each plan has its own separate features.

Eligibility requirements determine which employees can participate. These requirements may specify age, length of service, hours of service per year, and class of employee eligible for participation.

Contributions an employer or employee can make to a tax-favored retirement plan may be limited to a fixed dollar amount or percentage of compensation. The amount of contribution by the company is even more regulated. There are limits on contributions on behalf of both the individual employee and the total contribution to the entire plan.

"Vesting" is the percentage of an individual's retirement that can no longer be forfeited at a given time. As the employee's length of service increases, the percentage of vesting in the retirement account increases until the employee is entitled to 100 percent of the amount the employer contributed to his or her account.

Individuals who terminate employment before becoming 100 percent vested forfeit the unvested portion of their retirement benefits. These remaining funds stay in the plan and are reallocated among other participants or may be used to reduce employer contributions. This depends on the terms of the plan.

Some pension plans have provisions that allow employee contributions. They may be required in some plans and elective in others. Sometimes employee contributions are matched in whole or in part by the employer. Although employee contributions generally are made on an after-tax basis (401k and 404c plans are exceptions), earnings on these employee contributions can accumulate on a tax-deferred basis in a pension plan. Employees are fully vested on amounts they have contributed.

Most pension plans provide that benefits may be distributed to a plan participant upon retirement, termination of employment, or medical disability. Profitsharing plans may provide for distributions while the participant is still working. In death, distributions can be made to a designated surviving beneficiary. Distribution of benefits before age fifty-nine and a half are usually subject to a 10 percent penalty tax.

A retirement plan participant may receive pension benefits under certain circumstances before fifty-nine and a half and "roll it over" into an IRA. A rollover delays the tax consequences until the individual receives distributions.

To do this, the funds in the pension plan *must be transferred directly from one transfer agent to another.* Previously, when a person quit or was discharged from a job, he could take the money and use it for sixty days before establishing a new IRA. In 1992, Congress, in its "wisdom," decided that if an individual did this they should have 20 percent of it withheld. Further, if the person is under fifty-nine and a half the 10 percent tax penalty for early withdrawal should apply. If you should still choose to do this, you must submit proof that you replaced the monies into an IRA and apply for a tax refund. In essence, you will be giving the federal government a tax-free loan.

The tax treatment of the payout options vary depending on the reason for their distribution, the period over which the distribution is made, and whether or not the employee contributed to the plan.

Tax laws allow participants who were born on or before January 1, 1936, the options of five- or ten-year income averaging on lump sum distributions. Those born after that date have only the option of five year averaging once—after they reach fifty-nine and a half.

To summarize, pensions provide individuals a foundation for financial security at retirement. In a tax-favored plan, money accumulates on a tax-deferred basis until it is paid out at retirement or as a death benefit. Benefits paid at retirement may be taxed under special advantageous rules.

For the business, tax-favored pensions provide savings by providing an immediate tax deduction. It answers a growing need to improve employee benefits. A retirement plan rewards valuable employees. It encourages loyalty, productivity, and longevity. It may help attract better, more qualified employees. Finally, a pension plan is a means of funneling business dollars for personal benefit.

KINDS OF RETIREMENT PLANS (Tax-Favored)

There are many types of retirement plans. The simplest available for individuals who do not participate in a company plan is known as the **Individual Retirement Account (IRA).** An individual may set aside up to $2,000 or 100 percent of compensation, whichever is less, per year in an IRA. Further, if the individual contributes on behalf of a spouse who does not have compensation or elects on their joint federal tax return to be treated as having no compensation, the limitation is increased to $2,250 of compensation.

Some people are eligible to deduct their contributions to

an IRA. Individuals who are covered by certain employer-maintained retirement plans must meet the following adjusted gross income (AGI) requirements to qualify for this deduction:

AGI on single returns		AGI on joint returns
Under $25,000	Full deduction	Under $40,000
$25,000–$35,000	Deductions phased out	$40,000–$50,000
>$35,000	No deduction	>$50,000

Some words of caution about using IRAs as the sole means of retirement income planning are in order. Under current tax law IRAs may be subject to creditors. Further, if the IRA holder dies prematurely, the IRA may be subject to IRD (income received by the deceased). In other words the IRA becomes subject to ordinary income taxes—even before other distributions are made. If more than $150,000 is in the account, this becomes subject to a 15 percent excise tax as well. IRA post-mortem withdrawals are also subject to generation-skipping taxes and early withdrawal penalties.

Tax-sheltered annuities and custodial accounts (403[b] plans) are available to employees who work for a public educational institution or an organization designated as a 501(c)(3) by the Internal Revenue Service. These are tax-exempt organizations operated exclusively for charitable, religious, or educational purposes described by the IRS.

Under a 403(b) plan, eligible employees can contribute before-tax dollars to a plan through a salary reduction. Federal taxes are postponed until benefits are received. Maximum employee contribution is $9,500 (1991).

All contributions to a 403(b) plan are considered employer monies. An employer may make direct contributions to a 403(b) plan in addition to the employee's regular compensation or through a salary reduction agreement. When a salary reduction agreement is used, employee salary reduction monies are technically regarded as employer contributions.

Government-deferred compensation plans (457) are available to independent contractors and employees who provide services to a state or its subdivisions and their agencies or instrumentalities. Tax-exempt rural electrical cooperatives or any other tax-exempt organization other than governmental units are included.

Eligible participants may choose to contribute through salary reduction or bonus directly to a deferred compensation plan. These contributions are made before tax dollars. The tax-exempt entity retains ownership of the funds until they are distributed. Distributions are *not* eligible for rollovers to an IRA or for forward averaging when received.

Pension plans provide a valuable employee benefit. When plans are properly designed, both the employer and employee receive substantial tax benefits. These are called **qualified plans.** Qualified plans are divided into two categories—**defined benefit** and **defined contribution.** Both types are available to sole proprietors, partnerships, and corporations. The rules governing these plans are identical for both corporate and self-employed (Keough Plans) plans.

When an employer establishes a defined benefit plan, he agrees to pay a retirement benefit that is specified in the plan in advance. The amount specified is determined as a percentage of the employee's salary for the five years before retirement. Actuarial computations must be made each year to decide how much the employer must contribute for each employee. In that way the employee is reassured that there will be adequate funds available to pay the specified benefit at the time of retirement.

With defined contribution plans the employer puts aside a percentage of each eligible employee's salary. The percentage may be specified in the plan or fluctuate from year to year. In either case, the employee knows how much is contributed each year. Unlike the defined benefit plan (in which the employee knows how much he will receive at retirement), the amount that the employee receives at retirement with a defined contribution plan is determined by the amount in the employee's account. Therefore, if investments have been good, he will receive more. If not, he will receive less.

Another tax-favored retirement plan is called a **money purchase plan.** When this kind of plan is established, the employer must contribute an amount equivalent to a percentage of each eligible employee's compensation. This is a required contribution. The same percentage must be made on an annual basis. Maximum contribution is the lesser of 25 percent of compensation or $22,500.

Profitsharing plans offer employers much flexibility. Though only a contribution of the lesser amount of 15 percent income or $22,500 can be made, the percentage can vary from year to year. Unlike money purchase plans, contributions are not required. Profitsharing plans can be used with 401(k) and 404(c) plans.

In 1993 age-adjusted profitsharing plans became available. These allows older employees to have greater amounts set aside than younger employees. The theory is that older employees have less time to save for their retirement. Unlike their target benefit plans, annual contributions are not mandatory.

Employee stock ownership plans invest some or all of its assets in the securities of the employer. As with profitsharing plans, contributions can vary from year to year.

401(k) and 404(c) plans or **CODA** (cash or deferred arrangement) plans give the employee the option of electing to have the employer contribute an amount to a company retirement plan or to receive the amount in cash. If the employee chooses to contribute to a 401(k) plan, the employer may add a matching contribution. 401(k) contributions are deductible by the company. In addition, the contribution is not taxed to the employee as current income, because it is deferred compensation.

In 1994 plan participants began to direct their own investments. This relieves fiduciaries from liability for the investment decisions of participants who choose this option. At least three investment options must be offered in order to satisfy the "broad range of investments" required. Investment decisions must be permitted no less frequently than quarterly and more frequently if required by market volatility. The plan provider must make enough information about the investments available to participants so they can make informed choices. (The plan may make reasonable charges for the expense of providing this information, but this must be disclosed.) Finally, the plan must identify the fiduciaries who are obligated to provide this information and who will carry out the individual instructions.

One final note: The fiduciary, though exempt from liability of investment decisions made by the participant, is still liable for acts of ommission or fiduciary error.

Thrift (and savings) plans require employee contributions as a condition for participation. Frequently, the employer will match employee contributions on a dollar-for-dollar basis. Sometimes another matching formula is used. Employees can contribute between 1 percent and 6 percent of their income. Employer contributions to a thrift plan are deductible. Employee contributions are not.

Simplified Employee Pension plans or SEPs, as they are known, are individual retirement arrangements (account or annuity) that allow employers to contribute to their employee's IRAs. The employer is the plan administrator. Employer's contributions are tax deductible. Once the employer contributes for each eligible employee, each SEP account is treated like a traditional IRA.

Although the Internal Revenue Service treats this like a defined contribution plan, from certain aspects there are some important differences: a person cannot borrow from an SEP account, eligibility requirements are more liberal, the individual is 100 percent vested immediately, and, finally, government reporting requirements are minimal.

In 1986 the Tax Reform Act created another kind of SEP. This is known as a salary reduction **Simplified Retirement Plan.** Under this arrangement, employees may choose through salary reduction to defer a portion of their income into an SEP/IRA. This is similar to a 401(k) plan, but is geared to small business.

Target Benefit Plans are a hybrid of defined benefit and defined contribution plans. When it is established, the desired retirement benefit is identified. This is then converted to a specified contribution amount based on the employee's salary and an assumed rate of return. Unlike a profitsharing plan, the contribution amount on a target benefit plan is mandatory each year. Employer contributions are required. Contributions increase each year as the employee's salary and age increase. As a defined contribution plan, employees receive whatever is in their accounts at retirement. Maximum contribution to this kind of plan is the lesser of 25 percent of compensation, or $22,500. This type of plan should be used only with established businesses with a steady cash flow.

Some other things to keep in mind about funding-qualified pension plans: Only 50 percent of contributions to defined contribution plans may be allocated to purchasing whole life insurance; No more than 25 percent of contributions may be used to purchase term insurance or universal life insurance; In defined benefit plans, the face value of the policy must not be equal to a hundred times the monthly benefit at retirement. Still, this is one way of buying life insurance with tax-deductible dollars.

PENSION PLAN SPECIFICATIONS

Defined Benefit Plan
Type of organization: Incorporated and unincorporated businesses
Eligibility: Employees age 21, provide at least 1000 hours of service per year and have 1–3 years of service with company, depending on plan
Maximum annual deductible contribution: Amount needed to fund benefit; may be up to 100% of participant's average compensation for three years, or $112,221 (1992)
Obligation to contribute: Employer must meet minimum funding requirements
Vesting requirements: Graded vesting schedule, or 100%
Tax treatment of distributions: Lump sum distributions may be eligible for forward income averaging or rollover into IRA (BEWARE: AFTER JANUARY 1, 1993, THIS MUST BE DONE BETWEEN TRANSFER AGENTS FOR ALL PENSION PLANS. FAILURE TO DO SO MAY RESULT IN TAX WITHHOLDINGS AND PENALTY)
Typical funding: Conservative mix of investments, if small. May be more aggressive if larger
Use of insurance: Yes
Business profile: Key employees over 45; large amounts of recurring excess cash flow

Target Benefits Plans
Type of organization: Incorporated or unincorporated
Eligibility: Employees at least 21 years old, provide 1000 hours of more of service annually, and have 1–3 years of service

Maximum contribution: Up to 25% of eligible pay up to $22,500 per individual; employer limit is 25% of payroll
Obligation to contribute: Employer must make level annual contribution based on each employee's compensation
Vesting: Graded vesting, or 100%
Tax treatment of benefit of distributions: Forward averaging on lump sum distribution or rollover into IRA
Funding: Fairly conservative mix of investments
Use of insurance: Yes
Business profile: Older key employees, mature businesses with stable cash flow, more sophisticated qualified plan needs

Money Purchase Plan
Type of organization: Incorporated or unincorporated
Eligibility: Employees age 21 who provide at least 1000 hours of service annually with the company and have been with the company for 1–3 years
Maximum contribution: 25% of eligible pay to $22,500 per individual, employer limit of 25% of payroll
Obligation to contribute: Mandatory
Vesting: Graded vesting schedule, or 100%
Funding: Mix of conservative investments
Use of life insurance: Yes
Business profile: Younger key employees, mature businesses with stable cash flow, low employee turnover

Profitsharing Plan
Type of organization: Incorporated or unincorporated
Eligibility: Employees age 21 who provide at least 1000 hours of service with the company for 1–3 years
Maximum contribution: 15% of eligible pay up to $22,500 per individual; employer limit of 15% of eligible payroll
Obligation to contribute: Employer contribution is flexible; it may be voluntary and can change each year
Vesting: Graded vesting schedule, or 100%
Funding: Mix of conservative investments
Use of insurance: Yes
Business profile: Younger key employees, businesses with fluctuating profits, high employee turnover
Tax treatment of benefit distributions: Lump sums may be eligible for forward averaging or rollover to IRA

Thrift Plan
(Same as profit sharing)
Business profile: Younger key employees; employer has less cash

available for contributions; employer believes in value of employee participation in the plan

Employee Stock Option Plan
Plan requirements are similar to profit sharing. On certain occasions contributions may be greater than profit sharing. Contributions are in the form of stock in the company.

401(k) & 404(c) Plans (Cash or Deferred Arrangements CODAs)
Type of organization: Incorporated or unincorporated
Eligibility: Employee at least 21; 1000 hours of annual service to company; 1–3 years employment
Maximum contribution: 15% of individual's salary ($8894 in 1993); must be used with either a profitsharing or money purchase plan; maximum contributions for combination cannot exceed 25% of eligible compensation
Obligation to contribute: Individual makes pre-tax contributions, employer may match
Vesting: Immediately, 100% to the participant
Tax treatment of distributed benefits: Special tax treatments available on eligible lump sum distributions
Use of life insurance: Yes
Business profile: Growing business; employer has concern about contribution costs; large percentage of highly paid employees; employee base broad enough to pass discrimination tests.

Simplified Employee Pensions (SEPs)
Type of organization: Incorporated or unincorporated
Eligibility requirements: Any employee who is at least 21 years old with service for any part of three of the last five plan years who has earned at least $385 (1993) of compensation for the current plan year; this amount is adjusted each year to compensate for inflation.
Maximum annual contribution: 15% of compensation, up to $22,500
Obligation to contribution: Employer makes discretionary contributions
Vesting: Immediately, 100% to the participant
Tax treatment of benefit distributions: Distributions are treated as ordinary income in the year received; special forward averaging is *not* available
Use of life insurance: No
Business profile: Young key employees; small business with few employees; low employee turnover; few part-time or seasonal workers

Salary Reduction SEPs
   Type of organization: Incorporated or unincorporated
   Eligibility: Any employee who is at least 21 years with service for any part of three of the last five years who has earned at least $385 (1993) of compensation for the current plan year. This amount is adjusted each year to compensate for inflation.
   Maximum annual contribution: Up to $8,994 (1993) elective salary reduction contribution; employers may make discretionary contributions
   Obligation to contribute: Individual makes voluntary salary reduction contributions; these can be changed or discontinued from year to year
   Vesting: Immediately, 100% to participant
   Tax treatment of distributed benefits: Distribution are treated as ordinary income in the year received; forward income averaging is *not* available
   Business profile: Small businesses (fewer than 25 employees); low employee turnover; few part-time or seasonal workers; employees have discretionary income to make contributions
   Use of life insurance: No

457 Plans
   Type of organization: States and subdivisions of states and tax-exempt non-governmental organizations
   Eligibility: Any employee of a qualified organization
   Maximum annual contribution: Lesser of $7,500, or 25% of salary
   Obligation to contribute: Individual makes voluntary salary reduction contributions; they may change or discontinue each year
   Vesting: All 457 plans belong to the employer, subject only to the employer's general creditors
   Tax treatment of benefit distributions: Distributions are treated as ordinary income in the year received; special forward averaging is *not* available
   Use of life insurance: No
   Funding: Determined by state law

TSAs, TSCAs
   Type of organization: Public schools and 501(c)(3) organizations
   Eligibility: Any employee of a qualified organization
   Maximum contribution: $9500 (elective salary reduction)
   Obligation to contribute: Individual makes voluntary salary reduction contribution that can change or discontinue each year
   Vesting: Immediate 100%

Tax treatment of distributions: Distributions are treated as ordinary income in the year received; forward averaging *not* available
Funding: TSAs, annuities; TSCAs, mutual funds
Use of life insurance: No

IRAs
Type of organization: Individuals
Eligibility: Any wage earner under 70$^1/_2$
Maximum contribution: Up to $2,000 for individuals not covered by certain employer-maintained retirement plans; this amount is $2.250 for spousal IRAs; the deductible amount depends on their federal adjusted gross income and filing status
Obligation to contribute: None
Vesting: 100%
Tax treatment of distributions: Ordinary income in year received; *no* forward income averaging
Funding: Mutual funds, certificates, annuities, stocks, bonds, limited partnerships, U.S. gold coins, etc.
Use of life insurance: No

If as an employer you should decide to use a qualified retirement plan, the Department of Commerce and the Internal Revenue Service require that you have an investment policy statement. An example of this is as follows:

INVESTMENT POLICY STATEMENT
FOR
_____

The statement of investment goals and objectives is set forth according to the fiduciary responsibilities generally placed upon retirement plan sponsors. Its purpose is to express the Plan's position regarding asset allocation and relative investment performance.

1) The Plan intends to pursue a long-term investment objective of
_____
_____

2) The Plan expects to earn an average nominal rate of return over time of
_____ %

3) The Plan will compare returns over time to a mix of the following market indices:
   _____% S&P 500 _____% U.S. Treasury Bills
   _____% Shearson Lehman Bond Index
   _____% Dow Jones Industrial Average

4) The Plan expects to earn over time an average rate of return above the prevailing inflation rate of _____%.

5) The Plan believes that over time an appropriate target mix of assets would be:
   ___% GIC ___% Fixed Income ___% Balanced
   ___% Real Estate ___% Equity ___% Tangible
   ___% Oil & Gas ___% Other

6) The Plan will maintain reserves in a liquid assets fund to meet liquidity needs as necessary.

7) The Plan will have an investment horizon of _____ years.

8) The Plan will be reviewed on a _____ basis.

9) Other Plan Assumptions:
   ____% Inflation   ____% Liquidity
   ____% Tax Bracket   ____% Volatility

These goals and objectives are deemed to be appropriate for the _____ Retirement Plan. This policy will be communicated to all outside parties who will have investment control over plan assets.

_____Client   Date_____
_____Advisor   Date_____

References

Damico, Nicholas P., Esq., "Retirement Distribution Planning: New Developments," National Conference, 1992, Denver, Colorado.

Forbes, Fred A., "Pension Investing," National Conference, 1990, Denver, Colorado.

Johnson, Donald, "Investment Strategies During Retirement," *Personal Financial Planning*, September–October, 1992, pp. 7–10.

Larson, Allen, and Weishair, "Lawco Report," September, 1993, St. Paul, Minnesota.

Leimberg, Stephen R., McFadden, "The Tools and Techniques of Employee Benefit and Retirement Planning," 3rd Edition, 1993, National Underwriter, Cincinnati, Ohio.

Lesser, Gary S., J.D., "SEP's, SAR-SEP's, and 401k's Made Simple," National Conference, 1992, Denver, Colorado.

Pond, Jonathan, CPA, "Financial Planning Update," July, 1993, Denver, Colorado.
Sharkey, Eileen M., CFP, "Retirement Planning: Financial and Psychological Issues," National Conference, 1992, Denver, Colorado.
Steiz, Harry F., ChFC, CLU, "Tax Implications of Employee Benefits," National Conference, 1990, Denver, Colorado.
Temkin, Bruce J., MSPA, EA, "Qualified Plan Design," National Conference, 1990, Denver, Colorado.
Weisman, Herbert N. Weisman, D.D.S., CFP, "Retirement Planning for Dentists," *North West Dentistry*, January–February, 1991, pp. 55–56.
White, Joseph, CPA, Retirement Planning Worksheet, Personal Correspondence.

16 Nonqualified Deferred Compensation Plans

Sometimes employers establish nonqualified deferred compensation plans to avoid meeting Internal Revenue Service requirements for qualified plans. When properly set up, contributions made by the employer will result in a tax deferral on the deferred amount for the employee until they are actually received by the employee. Then the employer receives the tax deduction. There is no option of forward income averaging on lump sum distribution for the employee.

As indicated above, nonqualified deferred compensation plans need not conform to any IRS requirements for qualified plans. There are no government reporting requirements. Because of this feature, nonqualified plans can be structured in a variety of ways to meet the needs of the employer. Many nonqualified deferred compensation plans are "informally" funded with life insurance.

Supplemental executive retirement plans (SERPs) are established to provide additional retirement benefits to key employees. While qualified plans limit the maximum contribution an employer can make for an employee's benefit, SERPs can provide an extra layer of benefit beyond the company's pension plan and Social Security.

In purely nonqualified retirement plans, employer contributions are considered deferred compensation. With SERPs, employer contributions do not technically represent the current salary that has been deferred. It is, in essence, a bonus.

SERPs are not subject to the nondiscrimination requirements that are placed on qualified plans. They are offered to a select group of key executives who make significant contributions to the company's success. Because of certain tax considerations, SERPs are usually funded on a current disbursement basis. There is no limit on contributions.

If an employee should end his position before retirement, he forefeits his benefit in a SERP. There is usually no vesting in this type of plan. Distributions from a SERP are often paid monthly over the lifetime of the retired executive. Since distributions from a SERP are not eligible for five-year income averaging, benefits are rarely distributed in a lump sum.

Annuities can be used for a variety of retirement purposes. They can be qualified or nonqualified. When used as a funding vehicle for a qualified plan, the premiums are deductible to the employer. Used as a supplement to company pension plans they are usually not deductible. In either case, the income builds up on a tax-deferred basis.

Like qualified plans, annuities cannot be distributed until age fifty-nine and a half without incurring a penalty. If benefits are received before that time there is a 10 percent early withdrawal penalty for taxes. Furthermore, the insurance company may impose a penalty for early withdrawl during the first six or seven years for administrative costs. This usually decreases each year. In addition, you must begin making withdrawals from an annuity beginning at age seventy and a half.

Annuities can be flexible pay by installment or single pay. For people who are retired, it is possible to buy a single pay immediate annuity. This affords people an opportunity to have professional management of their money and be guaranteed an income for a specified period or life.

Payout options can be as follows:

Life income: This gives the annuitant monthly income for his/her life. There is no payout after he/she dies.

Life income with period certain: This provides monthly income during the life of the annuitant with a guarantee that payments will be made for 5, 10, 15 or 20 years.

Life income with installment "refund" period certain: This is similar to the above. The difference is that if the annuitant should die before the "period" specified, the payment will continue to be made to a named beneficiary for the period specified.

Joint and survivor life income: Monthly payment will be paid during the lifetime of the annuitant and joint annuitant.

Installments for specified period: A fixed dollar annuity will be payable monthly for a specified time. A period of 10–30 years may be selected.

17 Managing Assets During Retirement

During the 1980s, interest rates were historically high. Many retirees got used to receiving high rates of return on fixed interest rate investments with very little risk. At the beginning of the 1990s the economy turned sluggish. In response to this downturn, the Federal Reserve Bank lowered interest rates dramatically to stimulate the economy. Suddenly, many retirees began to get interest rate shock as their CDs began to mature. In short, their incomes declined sharply.

Because of this rapid decline in interest rates, many retirees panicked. Having fewer dollars to spend, many were forced to dip into the principal of their savings to meet current living expenses. For many retired people, invading their savings is traumatic. They worry that they may out live their savings. So what should a retired person do to minimize this sharp fluctuation in income?

PORTFOLIO MANAGEMENT

First, people must realize that inflation has been with us, with few exceptions, since 1776. Therefore, making investments based only on the current interest rate paid decreases future purchasing power and creates the panic situation mentioned above. The keys to stabilizing income and cash flow are **diversification** and **portfolio management.**

The essence of portfolio management is to balance the risk and return of the investments for each person's comfort level. Too many investors think of portfolio management as getting the highest current rate of return, thereby setting themselves up for poor results in the future. They choose either to not understand the risks involved or to ignore them.

Diversification is the key element of portfolio management. It addresses the issue of risk. Diversification involves more than just buying several different stocks. (Owners of mutual funds found this out the hard way in October, 1987, when the stock market took a nosedive.) It means that several different kinds of securities—for example, stocks, bonds, certificates of deposit, annuities, and other investments—should be considered. When one or two with diversification falter, the others can pick up the slack.

Obviously, if an investor could predict the asset class that would have the best performance each year, the highest returns could be obtained. Since no one has developed this ability, spreading the risk over various asset areas seems the best alternative.

Since most personal expenses occur monthly, many retirees prefer their cash inflows monthly. Cash inflows are often narrowly defined as income. A more accurate description would be income plus (in some situations) a return of principal. In any case, it is still cash retirees can spend.

As mentioned, many retirees are reluctant to spend their principal for fear of running out of money in later years. While this is understandable, a well-constructed plan can minimize the likelihood of spending too much principal. A balance can be made between investments that pay only income and those that return some principal. To summarize, although retirees should not be frivolous in spending their principal, they should not avoid it at all costs.

There is one reassuring point for retirees, the Plus One rule. What this means is that a person can draw income at 1 percent interest more than the current yield. By doing so, it will take twenty-nine years to use up all of the money. If the person should draw 2 percent above their rate of return, it will still take twenty years to use all of the money. Don't forget that remaining funds still draw interest.

In constructing **a portfolio for retired people,** four types of investment vehicles that provide monthly income should be included: **fixed annuities, government-backed securities, staggered utility stocks, and mutual funds.** Let us look at each of these briefly to see how they help to provide monthly income.

Fixed annuities provide a fixed monthly income that lasts as long as the retiree lives. If a joint and survivorship income option is used, the retiree can ensure a continuous cash flow after his or her death for as long as the spouse lives. This option leaves no money for other beneficiaries, but it does provide an income that the retiree and spouse cannot outlive. The financial strength of the insurance company issuing the annuity should be beyond question.

Government National Mortgage Association securities, or GNMAs, are securities backed by mortgages. The principal and interest on these are passed through to the investor. Payment of the principal and interest is guaranteed by the U. S. Government. The major risk of GNMAs is that a decrease in interest rates can cause prepayment of mortgages to increase. This risk can be minimized by purchasing existing GNMAs that sell at a discount.

Staggered utility stocks pay quarterly dividends and can provide reasonable current income with the prospect of increased dividends in the future. Three stocks can be selected that together stagger dividends to provide monthly income. For example, Stock A pays a dividend in January, Stock B in February, and Stock C in March. This then would repeat in each quarter. These stocks should be selected based on the company's financial soundness and potential for future dividend increases.

Mutual funds can provide monthly cash flow in two ways. First, mutual funds pay monthly income dividends. Second, the withdrawal plans offered by almost all funds can pay a monthly distribution of an amount designated by the retiree. Depending on the amount selected and the kind of fund chosen, it may be necessary for the fund to pay part of the principal. If the rate of withdrawal is less than the total return the fund earns, the principal will never be depleted.

By using various types of mutual funds, diversification is provided. This can stabilize monthly income in an economic environment environment of rising or falling interest rates.

During periods of falling interest rates, considerable reinvestment risk occurs for many retirees. As interest rates drop, the principal must be reinvested at lower rates of return. If a considerable amount of the retiree's portfolio matures simultaneously, his cash flow will be reduced accordingly. This, in turn, reduces his standard of living.

Assume that the investments already discussed are owned during falling interest rates. The monthly cash flows are affected as follows:

Fixed annuities: Cash flow remains the same.
GNMAs: Cash flow increases somewhat as prepayments increase. This is not necessarily desirable, because principal is dissipated at a faster rate.
Staggered utility stocks: Cash flow increases as dividends increase.

Mutual Funds:
Short-term bond fund: Cash flow will decrease as maturing bonds are reinvested in lower coupon bonds.
Intermediate term bond fund: Cash flow will decrease a lesser amount for the same reason.
Stock funds: Cash flow remains the same (fixed dollar amounts).

During times of increasing interest rates, these same investments perform as follows:

Fixed annuities: Cash flow remains the same.
GNMAs: Cash flow stays somewhat stable as payments decrease.

Staggered utility stocks: Cash flow increases as dividends increase.

Mutual Funds:
Short-term bond funds: Cash flow increases with maturing bonds and higher coupon bonds.
Intermediate and long-term bond funds: Cash flow increases some for the same reason.
Stock funds: Cash flow remains the same (fixed dollar amounts).

It should be noted during periods of changing interest rates that principal fluctuations will occur in each investment except the fixed annuities. On balance, these fluctuations should have little impact on retiree's cash flow. If only income is taken from the utility stocks and bond funds, principal fluctuations should be irrelevant. Yet, retirees should be aware that these fluctuations do occur and not panic.

Principal fluctuations from the stock funds over time work to the advantage of the retiree. Historically, stock funds have out-performed the rate of inflation. This growth is very important. As these funds appreciate, larger dollar withdrawals can be taken to maintain purchasing power without dissipating the original cash flow.

ASSET ALLOCATION

The next question to ask is the best mix of investments a retiree should choose. The answer depends on what risk tolerance each person has. Generally, retirees should have 70–80 percent in income investments and 20–30 percent in growth investments.

COMMON PITFALLS

There are some common mistakes that are often made by retirees investing their money. Frequently, they will put a large sum of money into an investment with a high current yield that also has a high risk. Many retirees make this mistake during times when interest rates are falling. It is an attempt to maintain their income level. One example of this is investing in junk bonds that have a lower credit rating but a higher yield.

A second mistake people tend to make is to be too concerned about safety. They invest in a portfolio of certificates of deposit, U. S. Treasury securities and savings accounts. This kind of portfolio has significant inflation risk. A man sixty-five years old has a life expectancy of seventeen more years. A woman sixty-five years old may live an additional 18.8 years. If inflation averages 5 percent per annum, a retiree's purchasing power will be cut in half in fourteen years. That is why it is important to have some common stocks to counter inflation.

A third mistake made by investors is insufficient diversification. As mentioned above, the "can't miss" type of investment can result in too large an investment relative to the whole portfolio. Some examples of these "can't miss" types of investments that failed are limited partnerships of the early 1980s and junk bonds of the late 1980s.

To conclude, remember that a well-structured portfolio needs to have a sensible balance between risk and return. It should provide adequate cash flow in both rising and falling interest rate periods. Once established, only minor occasional adjustments should be necessary to provide a regular, reliable cash flow during retirement years.

18 Investments

Investments are the one area most people get excited about. When ever you go to a party, a business lunch, or almost any social event, people like to talk about their investments. Why? The answer is that many people want to impress others about their "wisdom" and how great a return they are getting. They are saying "I'm rich." The real question is, are they? Often, financial planners see people who have "invested" their money for the wrong reasons and end up losing everything. The most glaring example of this is the limited partnerships issued in the early 1980s. Investors bought these primarily to get tax "write-offs" that could offset their current income. They didn't look at what their true rate of return would be without the tax benefit. *Never ever make an investment without evaluating the return without the tax benefit.* The tax benefit should be the "frosting on the cake" and not the main course.

RISKS ASSOCIATED WITH INVESTMENTS

When most amateur investors make an investment, the first, and often the only thing they look at, is the amount of interest or dividend that they will receive. Seldom do they take the time to look at the risks associated with that investment. Either they fail to acknowledge the risk or chose to ignore the fact that with a higher rate of return, there is greater risk associated. This is a prescription for disaster.

There are five different risks associated with each investment. Some risks are controllable, some are not. They are: **marketability, purchasing power risk, financial risk, business risk** and **interest rate risk.**

The first thing that a professional investor looks at is **liquidity.** This is simply the possibility of getting **all** of your money out of the investment with short notice. Though not a risk in the traditional sense, this is mentioned because people often confuse liquidity with marketability. An example of this kind of investment might be a demand deposit or certificate of deposit at a bank.

The first kind of risk to consider is **marketability.** If there is not a ready market for your investment, you may not be able to sell it when you wish. Real estate is a good example of this. A building for sale today may have to wait 3–6 months or more before finding a willing buyer.

On the other hand, common stock has a high degree of marketability but not necessarily a high degree of liquidity. There is no guarantee that you will receive all your money back. This is because stocks go down as well as up.

The second type of risk is **purchasing power risk.** As indicated in the previous chapter, many people who are too concerned with safety only put their money in the bank because it is backed by the U. S. government. They fail to realize that in future years, inflation will eat up their purchasing power. These "safe" investments usually fail to keep up with inflation on an after-tax basis. The other irony is that the federal agencies that "insure" these accounts have less than one dollar in reserve for every one hundred dollars on deposit.

The third kind of risk to consider is **financial risk.** This is the mix of debt and equity used to finance a firm or property. The larger the proportion of debt used, the greater the financial risk. This is why it is important to examine the company's balance sheet very carefully. Be sure that there are ample

```
Excellent  ┌─┐    ┌─┐         ┌─┐
           │ │    │ │         │ │
Good       │ │    │ │         │■│
           │■│    │■│    ┌─┐  │■│
Poor       │■│    │■│    │■│  │■│
        Tax Savings Cash Flow Appreciation Safety
```

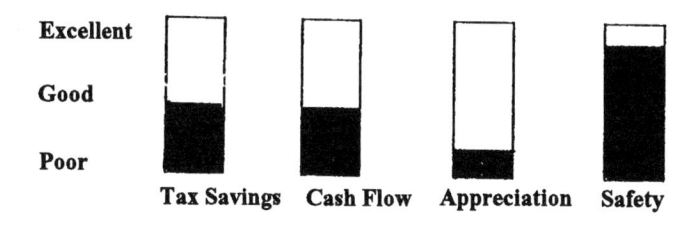

Figure 1

assets available for the company or property to service its long- and short-term debt.

The fourth risk is **business risk.** This is the risk associated with the nature of the business itself. This is concerned with the degree of uncertainty in the business's ability to pay its dividends, interest, and other debts due. Generally, it is believed that investments in like types of businesses have similar business risks. This is in spite of other factors, such as management and operating costs, that can play a roll.

Interest rate risk is caused by fluctuations in the general level of interest rates. This is especially true for investments that pay fixed periodic interest. To pay competitive rates of return, the principal of these securities decreases when interest rates rise and increases when interest rates fall. Examples of these are bonds, utility stocks, and preferred stocks.

Jim Jackson, a financial planner from Mount Pleasant, West Virginia, uses the "orange juice" example in his lectures to help people evaluate investment risk. He suggests that four glasses be labeled as follows: Tax savings; Cash flow; Appreciation; Safety. You then pour orange juice in each glass to the level that you believe answers each objective. Figure 1 shows how this would work for a high quality municipal bond.

Figure 2 illustrates the evaluation of a stock in a new company that is just coming to market.

After "pouring" the orange juice, it becomes obvious that buying a high-quality municipal bond has less risk for the reward offered than a stock issued for a new company. This

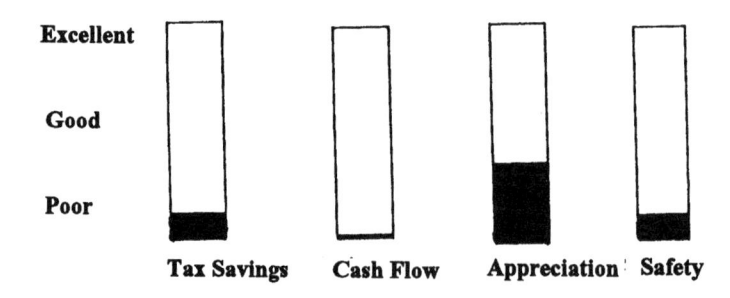

Figure 2

doesn't mean that you should not buy the stock. What it does mean is that you shouldn't put a large amount of your assets at risk on this type of speculation.

RULES FOR SUCCESSFUL INVESTING

Before diving into a discourse about successful investing, some terms need to be defined. **Investing** is puting money into an enterprise with the expectation of realizing a profit over a long period. **Speculation,** on the other hand, is putting money into an enterprise with the expectation of realizing a large gain in the short term. Generally, speculation involves a higher risk.

The first rule of successful investing is to do your homework. Do *not* take the word of a stockbroker or any other salesperson that the company or object you are buying into is sound. Read the prospectus and quarterly reports the company issues. If buying real estate or other property, get expert appraisal. I do not mean to disparage sales people. Most are honest, but they sell the "sizzle" and not the steak. It is your hope that you will make a profit from what they sell.

The second rule of successful investing is deciding what your objective is. If the investment meets your objective, and management is doing their job, stick with it. As an example, let us say that you want to buy a stock for income. So you buy a utility stock paying 6 percent dividend. If the stock was purchased when interest rates were low, the value of the stock will drop when interest rates rise. This is because their percentage of dividends must compete with other fixed income investments, not because the company is in trouble or worth less. If you understand that this is part of a cycle and that if the company continues to make a profit, the value of the stock will eventually rise, your objective of providing yourself with a reliable current income is still being met.

If your objective is to have small current income but capital appreciation, you would buy a "growth" stock. These stocks usually do not pay a high dividend, because most of the profits are reinvested in the company. Again, if management is doing its job well, you will profit.

If any investment does not meet your objectives, if there are flaws in management's performance, or external forces play a negative roll, cut your losses.

The third rule of successful investing is to diversify. The ancient Chinese traders learned centuries ago not to ship all their merchandise down the river to market in one ship. There was always the possibility that pirates would attack the ship or inclement weather could cause problems. We should learn from them to spread the risk.

When diversifying our investments, we should do so not only in terms of kinds of investments but also time. It is not possible for someone to predict market cycles with pinpoint accuracy. Therefore, when making investments, the payment should (if possible) be made over a long time span. An example of this is **income averaging.** This is frequently done with mutual funds.

The way this is done is as follows: The investor decides to put in the same amount of money each period. If during this period the value of the shares in the mutual fund goes up, the investor receives fewer shares. If their value goes down, the investor receives more shares. Over the long haul, inflation has caused the stock market to go up. So after a long period the investor will have more shares at a higher price.

The next rule of successful investing is never to invest more than you can afford to lose. Often, people will do this with the expectation of making a "quick buck." This seldom works out. Successful investing requires discipline and patience.

Finally, plan when you want to get out of the investment. When the market that your investment is in is going up, it is natural to try to ride it to the top of the cycle. There is a saying on Wall Street that "Bulls make money. Bears make money. Pigs get slaughtered." Don't get greedy. It is better to make a profit then to die broke.

The Business Cycle

Part of successful investing is understanding the business cycle. Economists divide the cycle into four parts. They are trough to recovery, recovery to expansion, expansion to peak, and peak to contraction.

During the trough-to-recovery period, gross national product (GNP), industrial production, capacity utilization, unit production costs, and the producer price index are down. Only labor productivity is up. This occurs because as business lays off workers, fewer workers are left to maintain production.

In the second phase, known as recovery to expansion, the consumer price index drops with unemployment. Simultaneously housing starts, mortgage debt, retail sales, automobile sales, and consumer credit increase.

As the economy finally takes off in the expansion-to-peak period, GNP, industrial production, capacity utilization, unit labor costs, and the producer price index increase while labor productivity decreases. This happens in expanding economic times as business adds more help in anticipation of increased business.

Eventually, phase four, peak to contraction, begins. Although the consumer price index and unemployment increase, mortgage debt, housing starts, retail and auto sales decline. Finally, the length of the average work week decreases.

Figure 3 illustrates the business cycle. Understanding this relationship is very important. For example, investors in common stocks have learned over the years that the stock market usually anticipates the business cycle by six to nine months. They make their stock selections in various sectors of the economy based on their judgment of how long each segment

Expansion Peak

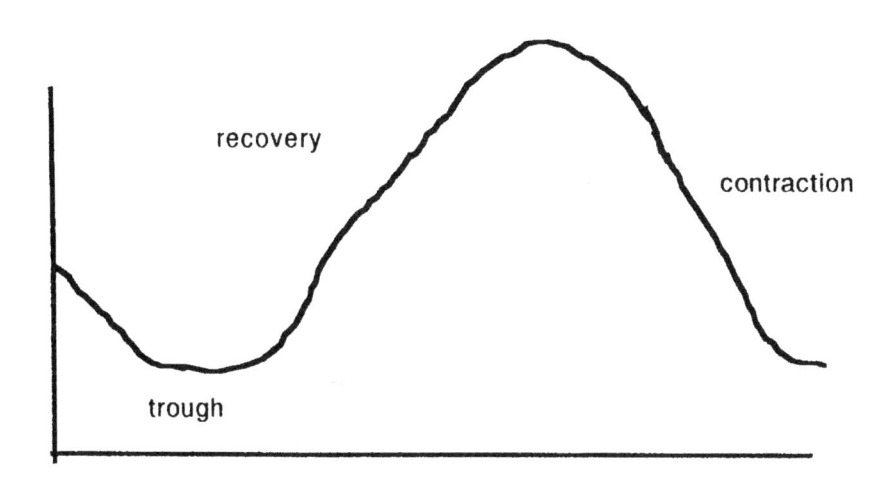

Figure 3

will last. Each analyst has his model. Table 1 is just one such example.

In the preceding paragraphs was a description of what happens to the leading economic indicators during the various stages of the economic cycle. Historically, boom times have lasted four times longer than recessions. So what does this translate to for you, the investor? In the following table, a buying strategy is presented as an example of when to buy certain investments. This should not be considered gospel. It is used by some analysts as a guess for the economic environment at the time. When you understand what potentials are for various investments, you will probably develop your own investment strategy.

A Buy-Sell Strategy During a Business Cycle*

	Trough	Recovery	Expansion	Contraction
Stocks				
Capital Goods	Buy	Buy		
Consumer Basic				Buy
Discretionary	Buy	Buy		
Finance	Buy	Buy	Buy	
General Business				Buy
Manufacturing	Buy	Buy		
Petroleum	Buy	Buy	Buy	
Shelter	Buy	Buy	Buy	
Transportation	Buy	Buy		
Utilities				Buy
Bonds				
Short-term			Buy	
Long-term				Buy
Speculative	Buy	Buy		
Good Quality				Buy
Convertible Bonds	Buy	Buy		
Collectibles	Buy	Buy	Buy	
Real Estate	Buy	Buy	Buy	
Strategies				
Puts	Sell	Sell	Buy	Buy
Calls	Buy	Buy	Sell	Sell
Futures	Buy	Buy	Buy	
Going Short			Yes	Yes
Buying on?				
Margin	Yes	Yes		

Table 1

*This was only one of several strategies presented by Jeffrey Koch, Vice President of Amerifirst Florida Trust Company, Boca Raton, Florida, at the 1988 financial planners convention.

References

Allaire, Keith D., MBA, "Limited Partnerships: Post Tax Reform," National Conference, Denver, Colorado, 1990.

Auerbach, Arthur, CPA, "Planning for the Upper Income Client," National Confrence, Denver, Colorado, 1991.

Cohen, Abby J., CFA, "Investment Planning: The Financial Market Place," National Conference, Denver, Colorado, 1992.

Cohen, Harry D., "Smart Investment Planning," National Conference, Denver, Colorado, 1991.

Economos, Andrew F., PhD, "Global Investment Opportunities," National Conference, Denver, Colorado, 1991.

Golden, Anne B., CFP, "Stocks and Bonds; Defensive Investing," National Conference, Denver, Colorado, 1990.

Jackson, Jim, D.D.S., CFP, "Managing Your Investments," ADA Seminar, Chicago, Illinois, 1985.

Johnston, Lawrence, F., DBA, CFP, CLU, ChFC, "Investment Aspects of Insurance," National Conference, Denver, Colorado, 1992.

Markese, John D., PhD, "Investing for Growth and Income," National Conference, Denver, Colorado, 1991.

Perrit, Gerald W., PhD, "Building and Maintaining an All Weather Portfolio," National Conference, Denver, Colorado, 1991.

19 Investment Vehicles

❦

What people invest their money in depends on their comfort level. It is important to remember that the greater the risk a person is willing to take, the greater the potential reward. The other side of the coin is that the greater the risk, the greater the possibility of losing money. The College for Financial Planning* in Denver, Colorado, prioritizes various investments by amount of risk as follows:

High Risk	Future contracts
	Speculative common stocks, collectibles
	Limited partnerships, real estate properties, puts & calls
	High-grade common stock, growth mutual funds
Reward	Balanced mutual funds, high-grade preferred stock,
Potential	High-grade convertible securities
	High-grade municipal bonds, high-grade corporate bonds, money market accounts
	U. S. insured checking and savings accounts, Treasury securities, life insurance cash values, EE and HH bonds,
Low Risk	U.S. low-risk insured certificates of deposit

Table 2

*The College for Financial Planning offers courses leading to the educational requirements necessary for certification by the International Board of Certified Financial Planners.

By now you should know that investing your money is not without some kind of risk. But not investing your money leads to the risk of losing purchasing power over the years. So let us look at some common investments.

Common Stocks

When an individual purchases shares of common stocks, he/she is buying a part ownership in the company. These shares are traded on an exchange. Examples of these are the New York Stock Exchange and the American Stock Exchange. Each exchange has its own requirements for membership in order for a company to be traded.

Common stockholders earn their return in two ways—growth and dividends. A shareholder's main concern is with the performance of the firm. This is its capacity to generate earnings (profitability). The price a stock trades at is based on a multiple of what investors feel future earnings will be. This is known as **price to earnings ratio (P/E).** Other concerns of common stock investors are payout ratios, earnings, and dividend growth.

Unless a firm derives its income from a portfolio, sales are the main source of revenues. The ability to generate profitable sales is indicated by profitability ratios such as gross profit margin (i.e., gross profit divided by sales).

The operating profit margin (earnings before interest and taxes, divided by sales) is also important. This may show specific areas where a firm excels or is having problems. By comparing changes in gross profit margin, operating profit margin, and net profits, these areas can be identified.

Dividends are usually paid to the shareholders on a quarterly basis. This is determined by the shareholder's record five days before the end of the fiscal quarter. This is because most stock trades are not finalized until payment for the order is due (five days after the transaction). The day after this is called the **x dividend**. This is listed in the stock section of the business newspapers.

One final note: Because common stockholders are part owners of the company, they share in the profitability and losses of the company. Although there is no transfer of liability to the individual, dividends may be increased in a good year or cut in a poor economic climate.

Preferred Stock

Like common stock, preferred stocks are an equity position in the company. Both are means for companies to raise operating capital. There are some significant differences.

Holders of preferred stocks do not have the right to vote (as common shareholders do) in matters of company policy. They do receive a fixed dividend. During times of economic hardship, a firm can omit its preferred dividend without becoming insolvent. When dividends are cumulative, any arrears of preferred dividends must be paid before common shareholders. That is where the name "preferred" is derived.

Preferred stocks do not have a maturity date but sometimes may be subject to call. This can happen if the fixed rate that they are paying out becomes higher than the current cost of money to the firm. It is interesting that some firms have a sinking fund established to pay their preferred dividends. This is usually required for bonds. Like bonds and other fixed income investments, the price of the preferred stock may be influenced by current yields for other equivalent investments.

Bonds

A bond is basically a loan. The company or governmental agency issues the bond to pay its long-term obligations. Bonds are issued because the amount of the obligation may be too large for a bank to handle on a long-term basis. Often, bonds are issued in series so that they mature at different intervals. The longer the interval, the higher the interest paid.

Some bonds are callable. This means that the issuer can call the bonds and pay them off earlier at a given price. This is done when the bond is issued at a higher interest rate and then interest rates drop. Frequently, the issuing party will sell new bonds at the prevailing interest rate and then call the older issue.

Issuers must maintain a *sinking fund,* a guaranteed repayment of the bonds. If a company goes "belly up," bond holders must be paid before stockholders from the company assets.

Investors should realize that *not* all bonds are created equal. Those issued by the United States Government are considered the safest. Others may have investment ratings from excellent to poor by the rating agencies.

There are two systems for rating bonds. These ratings range from "triple A" to C or D. The highest rated bonds by Standard and Poor's is AAA. The quality descends to AA, A, BBB, etc. The other system by Moody starts at Aaa, Aa, A, and proceeds to Baa, Ba, B, etc. Baa is considered the lowest grade of investment quality bonds.

There are many **kinds of corporate bonds. Mortgage bonds** are backed by a lien on the assets of the corporation. Most corporate bonds that are issued today are called **debentures.** They are backed by the full faith and credit of the corporation but have no special lien on the corporate assets. **Subordinate debentures** have a claim on corporate assets but only after claims on the previous bonds have been satisfied. A few bonds called **income debentures** pay interest only if it is earned.

Various kinds of **equipment trust certificates** (e.g., railroad equipment trusts) are considered high quality because of the direct claim on assets.

Deep Discount Bonds and Zero Coupon Bonds

Deep discount bonds are sold in the market for much less than their face value **(par value).** The reason for this is that when they were issued interest rates were lower. As an example, let's take a bond with a 5 percent coupon rate that matures in ten years. If we assume that the bond is selling for 72, it means that an investor will pay $720 for a $1,000 bond. This is a 28 percent discount from par.

Why would someone buy such a bond? There are several reasons for this. The first is that they provide automatic call protection. This is because their coupon may be low compared to current rates. Further, they have a built in capital gain. If the bondholder keeps the bond until maturity, he will receive the full $1,000. In the meantime he will have a reasonably good current yield. If the bond is held for long term, it will be taxed under a more favorable long-term capital gains rate.

Zero coupon bonds are original issue discount bonds. They are sold without any stated coupon rate and therefore without any current interest rate income. When sold, they are sold at a substantial discount from par value. In this way, the yield to maturity is guaranteed. For example, a $1000 par value that matures in ten years might be purchased for $150. At maturity, the bondholder will receive $1,000. In this way, high yields can be assured.

Because interest on zero coupon bonds is taxable each year, these bonds are generally only used in pension plans in which taxes are deferred. Municipal bonds can also be purchased as "zeroes."

Municipal bonds provide interest that is exempt from federal taxes and sometimes state taxes as well. Municipals are particularly attractive to people who are in a high tax bracket. To find the equivalent yield of a tax-free municipal bond with a taxable investment, all that is necessary is to divide the yield of the municipal bond by one, minus the tax bracket.

For example, let us assume that a municipal bond has a 6 percent yield and the investor is in the 28 percent tax bracket.

$$6\% / 1-.28 = 6\% / .72 = .082 = 8.2\%$$

If there is also a state tax, be sure to add this into the equation. If there were a 4 percent state sales tax, the equation would be

$$6\% / 1- .32 = .088 = 8.8\%.$$

Kinds of Municipal Bonds

There are several different kinds of municipal bonds of which the investor should be aware. The type of bond has an impact on the security behind it.

General obligation bonds are the largest category of municipal bonds. They are backed by the full faith, credit, and taxing authority of the issuing party. For example, if a state is the issuing authority, the state's money sources of revenue can be used to pay the principal and interest of the bond. Local municipalities derive their income from unlimited ad valorem taxes on all taxable property within the area. Sometimes an issuer will borrow funds, and pledge only a part of its taxing power for payment of principal and interest. These general obligation bonds are known as *limited tax bonds*.

Special tax bonds are payable only from the proceeds of a single tax, series of taxes, or another specific source of revenue. These obligations are not backed by the full faith and credit of the municipality.

Revenue bonds are issued to finance many different kinds of projects such as sewer, gas, electrical facilities, stadiums, hospitals, etc. The principal and interest are paid entirely from the revenues generated by these projects. Toll roads are the best known examples of this.

Other Important Information

Municipal bonds are bearer bonds. They may also mature serially. This means that some bonds in each issue reach maturity at different times. Although in a secondary market there exist more municipal bonds, most bonds are redeemable only at maturity.

Ratings of municipal bonds are provided by Moody's and Standard and Poor's rating services. Most municipal bonds are regarded, from a quality point of view, second to U. S. Government obligations.

Short-term tax free notes are issued by local agencies, states, municipalities, and other political subdivisions in denominations of $5,000 or more. They mature from one month to one year from date of issue. They are usually backed by the full faith and credit of the issuer. Some people in high tax brackets use these notes between other financial commitments.

Bond Funds

There are many types of bond funds available. Some operate in much the same way as **mutual funds,** and others operate as **unit investment trusts.** It is important to understand the difference.

Both types of funds buy many different issues of bonds. The difference between the two is that the bond fund that operates as a mutual fund has a managed portfolio. This means that the portfolio manager is constantly buying and selling the bonds to yield the greatest possible return to the investor. The price of the bond fund is determined daily by the total assets of the fund divided by the number of shares in the fund. They are traded on the open market and may be purchased by any investor at the current market price.

With unit investment trusts, the portfolio of securities is selected at the time the trust is organized, and not subsequently changed. The sponsor of the trust (usually a brokerage house or investment banker) then sells units of the trust to investors. There are no management or redemption fees in connection with these trusts. The value of the units are determined by the value of the bonds at the time of redemption. Unit investment trusts can be found with different qualities of bonds and different maturity dates to meet individual investors needs.

Bond funds may specialize in government bonds, corporate bonds, municipal bonds, or may be balanced with a variety of issues. Again, be reminded that those with the highest yields also may invest in bonds of poorer quality. This is not necessarily bad if there exists sufficient diversification to compensate if one or two issues go bad.

Other Fixed Income Obligations

United States Treasury obligations, savings bonds, certificates of deposit, and savings accounts have already been discussed in the chapter about savings. There are several other kinds of fixed income securities of which the investor should be aware. They are: **United States Government agency securities, flower bonds, Ginnie Mae pass-throughs,** and **commercial paper.**

United States Government agency bonds are issued by the United States Treasury, an agency of the United States Government. The agencies are the Federal Intermediate Credit Banks, the District Banks for Cooperatives, the Federal Land Banks, the Federal Home Loan Banks, the Federal National Mortgage Association (Fanny Mae), the Government National Mortgage Association, the International Bank for Reconstruction and Development (World Bank), and the Inter-American Development Bank.

These securities are rated in quality one step below United States Treasury securities. As such they usually pay one-half to one percent more the equivalent U.S. Treasury securities. Although the U. S. Government does not officially back these securities, Congress has shown enough moral sense to do so.

Flower bonds are United States Government bonds with a special feature. The federal government will accept them at full face value in payment of estate taxes. Although not issued anymore, they may be purchased at a discount on the secondary market until 1998.

Ginnie Mae pass-through securities permit an individual to earn high mortgage yields, with both principal and interest payments guaranteed by the federal government. Most of these securities mature in ten to twelve years. A minimum investment of $25,000 is required. It should be noted that part of the principal is returned with interest payments each month.

Commercial paper is the name given to short-term promissory notes of well-established corporate borrowers. A minimum amount of $10,000 is required. Commercial paper matures within nine months. It is usually sold on a discount basis.

REAL ESTATE INVESTMENT TRUSTS (REITs)

Although REITs are sold on stock exchanges, they operate very much like closed end mutual funds. It is one way the investor can invest in real estate and have the advantages of corporate ownership. This may include central management, limited liability, continuity of interests, and transferability of ownership.

REITs have an advantage over public real estate corporations from the tax point of view. Because they distribute their earnings to their shareholders, they are not taxed. The shareholders then pay tax on the distributions as ordinary income.

REITs come in several forms, from conservative to risky. The conservative forms maintain a high equity position. The risky REITs invest primarily in mortgages for their interest. Balanced REITs may have somewhat equal positions in both. Quality of management is most important.

OTHER FORMS OF REAL ESTATE INVESTMENTS

There are other forms of real estate investments of which you should be aware. Some are very speculative while others may be conservative. They are unimproved land and improved land.

Unimproved land can be a very risky investment. It is not in the scope of this book to discuss the detail of this type of investment.

Improved real estate comes in two forms—new and used residential property (apartment houses, etc.), namely, low income housing (for which investors have been allowed certain tax credits), and commercial real estate (such as office buildings, shopping centers, etc.).

A word of advice if you invest in real estate: real estate is a full-time business. It involves much expertise if the investor is to be successful. There are many lecturers on the circuit today telling "how you can make a million from scratch" in real estate. It is possible, but a great deal of time and knowledge is required.

OIL AND GAS VENTURES

Oil and gas ventures are by nature very risky. On the other hand, they can be very rewarding if your well "comes in."

Incentives for taxpayers in a high bracket to invest in such ventures include the sheltering of other income through tax deductions allowed for drilling costs and depreciation. Though people can invest directly in oil operations, registered limited partnerships are the easiest way to do this.

Similar to the oil and gas ventures are other tax shelters that invest in materials, such as cattle breeding, equipment leasing, and timber operations. These are very speculative, so beware.

PUT AND CALL OPTIONS

Trading in options to buy or sell common stock (calls and puts) has become a major speculative technique for many investors. Options are traded on the Chicago Board of Options Exchange as well as some smaller stock exchanges. The prices of options are quoted daily in the *Wall Street Journal* and many other daily newspapers.

Calls and Puts are options to buy and sell a given stock during a specific period at a given price. The price of the stock is known as the **strike** price. A call is an option to purchase a certain stock from someone at a given price anytime during a specific period. On the other hand, a put is an option for a seller to sell someone a given stock at a set price during a given period. Options are traded in round lots of 100 shares.

Normally, you will buy an option on a stock if you want to speculate that the stock is going to go up or down beyond certain limits. The price you pay for the option is known as the **premium.**

Let us look at how buying options might work. Suppose that you believe that the price of ABC stock is selling too low, and that its price will go up substantially in the near future. In this circumstance you might buy a call option to buy this stock at the present price. If the stock is selling for $62 per share on March 1, you would buy a call option (October 60) for $700 (plus commission) premium. This gives you the right to purchase 100 shares of stock at any time during this period for $62 per share.

Now suppose that you were right and the stock goes up to

$72 per share on June 1. This is three months before the option expires. The value of the option has now increased to $1300. You sell your option for $1300 and make $600 profit (less commissions) for that three-month transaction.

It becomes evident that $600 profit on a $700 investment is an 85 percent return. The price increase of the stock from $62 to $72 is only an 11 percent return. So there is considerable leverage with options.

You might have bought the stock outright and then sold it. But then you would have had to pay out more money for the stock. If you do not exercise your right to buy the shares during the specified period, you lose your premium.

Sophisticated investors use many techniques to trade in options. One such technique is called the **straddle.** Using this technique the investor buys a put and a call on the same stock at the same price for the same exercise period. Here the speculator will profit if the price goes far enough in either direction to offset both premiums paid.

Be aware that trading in options is highly speculative. Therefore, commit only a small percentage of your investment assets to this.

The other side of the option coin is selling (writing) options. This is done for an entirely different reason than buying a call. Suppose that as an investor you have bought a common stock that has appreciated substantially. Now you would like to increase your yield. So you sell a **put** for a given price. The increased yield comes from the premiums that the option writer receives on his option. The option writer also is entitled to all cash dividends paid on that stock, but the option writer must pay all commissions and transaction fees.

The option writer also gives up any possibility of further capital appreciation on the stock. If it should appreciate, it will be called away. If it should go down, the option writer bears the risk. He cannot sell the stock until the option expires (unless he is willing to take the chance that it can be repurchased at a lower price). This is highly speculative. When this is done, it is called going "naked."

Commodity Futures Trading

Trading in commodities is highly speculative. In some ways it is similar to buying stock options. A **futures contrast** is an agreement to buy or sell a commodity at a price stated in the agreement on a specified future date. While futures contracts call for the delivery of the commodity (unless the contract is liquidated before maturity), this is rarely done. Speculators usually "close out" their position before it matures. In this way, they never have to take delivery of the commodity.

Commodities are traded on the spot market. The financial pages of many daily newspapers list them. Often the margin requirements are minimal—5–10 percent of the value of the commodity. The actual trading is done in much the same way as buying puts, calls, and straddles.

There are many other techniques for dealing in commodity futures. They will not be discussed here. A broker or dealer can advise you if you are interested.

Commodity contracts are highly leveraged and very speculative. There are opportunities for extraordinary gains, but also for extraordinary losses. Unless you are involved in the commodities business, BEWARE of the possibility of going broke.

Collectibles

Collectibles consist of art, coins, gold, silver, etc. Many people like to invest in these more unusual items. People who "invest" in these items usually do this because they view these as a hedge against inflation. This is true only if their price is rising, and there is not necessarily a connection between the price of these items and inflation.

Buying these items requires specialized knowledge so it is important to know what you are doing. Because they produce no income, there are additional costs to storing and insuring them. Fortunately, many of these people enjoy the items that they collect, so it is logical for them to acquire these items.

Mutual Funds

The availability of so many different investment choices means that you need more information to identify which ones are right for your needs. Mutual funds have added a new dimension to investing, while they have created a bit of confusion. The reason for this is that there are so many, and each has its own objectives.

What are mutual funds? They are pooled investments. When you buy a share in a mutual fund, you are buying a partial ownership in a portfolio of professionally managed stocks, bonds, or other securities.

There are some fundamental differences between buying stocks and mutual funds. Purchasing stocks involves buying shares of an individual company. Usually, this is in **round lots** (100 shares). Sometimes individuals buy fewer than 100 shares. This is known as **odd lots.** When shares are sold in 1000 share units, it is known as a **block.** You cannot buy a fraction of a share. The price you pay is dictated by the stock's current market value.

A mutual fund, on the other hand, may invest in fifty or more different securities, providing built-in diversification. These may include stocks only, bonds, puts, calls, or any combination of them. The value you pay for a share of a mutual fund is the total value of the portfolio on a given day divided by the number of shares outstanding. After opening an account, you can invest almost any amount for a certain minimum amount. Because the fund is professionally managed, the portfolio manager decides which securities to buy or sell based on the fund's objectives. You decide when you wish to buy or sell your shares. Fractions of a share can be purchased.

There are several different **categories of mutual funds.** This is based on the primary objectives of the fund or the types of investments included in the fund. They are **aggressive growth funds, growth funds, growth and income funds, and income funds.**

Aggressive growth funds aim for maximum capital gains by investing in companies that have the highest growth potential. This may include young companies or those that are in volatile industries. These funds have a high degree of risk.

Growth funds invest for long-term capital gains in well-established companies and industries. They may carry a lower degree of risk than aggressive growth funds.

Growth and income funds offer the potential of moderate capital gains and moderate income with moderate risk. These funds may invest in companies with a track record of consistent dividends.

Income funds invest in securities that provide a high degree of income.

Mutual funds are also categorized as **open end funds** and **closed end funds.** Open end funds continuously issue new shares of stock in their portfolios. In this way the size and overall value of the fund grows and shrinks based on the number of shares outstanding. Closed end funds, on the other hand, have a fixed number of shares. Unlike the open end funds, the overall value of the fund is determined solely by the value of their portfolios and not by the value of the portfolio and the new shares influx. Closed end funds are traded on stock exchanges whereas open end shares are purchased directly from the company.

Some open end mutual funds charge a "load" and some are "no load" mutual funds. The "load" is the commission paid to the salesperson who sells you the fund. When you buy a load-type mutual fund, the commission is included in the "offer price." When you redeem these shares there is usually no commission. These shares are sold at net asset value (NAV).

Which fund should you buy? Over the long term, studies show that it makes no difference. The fact is that there is no such thing as a free lunch. The no-load funds often have a higher expense ratio than the load funds. Also many no-load funds have a rear end load. So they charge a percentage sales charge when you withdraw your funds. If the net asset value has increased over the years, the sales charge may be more than what the original commission might have been.

There is a "hidden" commission sometimes found in both types of funds. This is known as a **12 b-1** after the Security and Exchange Commission regulation. This allows mutual funds to take as much as 1 percent of your money for advertising and promotion purposes. If the fund does this it will be noted in the prospectus of the fund. I think this is a sham. Try to find a fund that does not have one.

What should you look for when buying a mutual fund? First, you will want to find a fund that meets your objectives. Obviously, you wouldn't buy a growth fund if your main objective was current income. Second, ask yourself how much risk you are willing to take. Professionals look at the **beta** of a stock or mutual fund. This is the amount of volatility of the fund. If the fund goes up or down at the same rate as the overall market, it is said to have a beta of 1.0. If is has a higher beta, it goes up or down faster than the market as a whole. It has more risk. Conversely, a fund that has a lower beta appreciates or depreciates more slowly. Bond funds usually have a lower beta. The risk of many funds can be found at the library in the *Value Line Index* or the *Mutual Fund Forecaster*. Third, it is wise to check the fund's management. What is their record for the past five years? Ten years? Is it the same management today as then? How have they done in up and down markets? Fourth, you should check the fund's portfolio. Would you want to own the securities in it? Finally, you might want to find out what shareholder services are available. Do they have the right of accumulation or an exchange privilege with other funds in their family? What about systematic withdrawals? Once you have this information, you can make a rational judgment whether or not to invest.

Mutual funds may be purchased by investing one lump sum, on a voluntary installment basis, or on a contractual basis. Lump sum and contractual basis of mutual fund are not recommended. If a person invests a lump sum when the market is high and it then drops, he will lose money. If a person invests on a contractual basis, up to 50 percent of the first year's investment may be a front end load. This leaves fewer dollars for investment.

Mutual fund investing should be viewed as a long-term investment. If a person makes regular period investments, they will **dollar cost average** their investments. To see the wisdom of doing this look at the chart below.

Month	Amount invested	Price/share	Number of shares
1	$100	$10	10
2	$100	$11	9.090
3	$100	$9	11.11
4	$100	$12	8.33
5	$100	$13	7.69
Total	$500	$11 (Avg Cost)	46.22

$11 (Avg Cost) × 46.22 = $508.42 Present Value

Over the long term the stock market trend has been up. As the chart shows, by making investments regularly, the probability of making a profit is very good. It is not as exciting as trying to out-guess the timing of the market, but it works. If the market should go down (heaven forbid), then the overall losses are less. This is because we are diversifying risk by investing evenly over time.

One advantage of mutual fund investing is that most offer a systematic withdrawal plan. After a certain minimum amount has been invested (usually $5000 or $10,000), specific monthly amounts can be paid to the investor over a period. This feature can be very valuable at retirement, or if a person should become disabled. It provides an additional source of income.

LIMITED PARTNERSHIPS

Limited Partnerships are used for many large investment purposes. They may be used to help finance real estate, equipment leases, cattle or horse breeding, and many other projects. They are called limited partnerships because the investors have limited liability if things go sour.

The way they work is that a person or company (known as the **general partner)** finds a property. Instead of going to a bank for financing, he forms a limited partnership with many individuals. Each **limited partner** buys units in the partnership. Often they are offered in $5,000 or $10,000 denominations. The general partner may take 10 percent or more for setting up the limited partnership. A brokerage firm may sell the units for a commission. At the initial offering it is customary for the general partner to pay the commission. The remaining funds are used to purchase the properties and for operations.

The general partner is also paid an annual fee for management of the properties. If the properties are sold before the limited partnership ends, the profits or losses are passed through to the limited partners. Frequently, the general partner will delay taking any profits until the limited partners get back their initial investment.

The limited partner gets any income that the properties generate as well as a proportional share of the depreciation. This may shelter some income from taxes. If the property is sold, he receives a share of the profits.

Before the Tax Reform Act of 1986, limited partnerships were highly leveraged. TFRA eliminated this tax preference (loophole). Consequently, many people have lost money in these investments. The lesson here is simple. Make your investments based on their rate of return and other aforementioned criteria, and not based on how much in taxes you will save.

Here are some other things to keep in mind when buying a limited partnership. First, remember that this is a very long-term commitment. Second, if some properties are sold before the partnership matures, there may be some recapture of the tax savings, i.e. the government may require you to pay taxes on the amount that you previously wrote off as depreciation. Third, limited partnerships are illiquid. So if you need your money before maturity, you may not get your money out. Finally, there is no ready market for many of these. Even for death, an estate may have problems liquidating.

TREASURY SECURITIES

Securities issued by the United States Treasury are considered the safest investments. Consequently, they carry the highest possible credit rating in all maturity ranges. Savings bonds have already been discussed in the chapter about savings.

Other United States Treasury instruments are Treasury Bills, Treasury Notes, and Treasury Bonds.

Treasury Bills are bearer obligations issued on a discount basis and redeemed at face value at maturity. Maturity dates are at three-month intervals up to one year. The minimum denomination of purchase is $10,000. At present, the Treasury offers two competitive bids each week. One is for three months, and the other is for six months. Each month the Treasury offers competitive bids for nine-month and one-year maturities. Noncompetitive bids for each issue in amounts of $10,000 to $200,000 may be submitted. This means that they will be accepted at the price accepted for competitive bids of the same issue.

Treasury Bills may be purchased through the bond department of most commercial banks, or directly from the Federal Reserve Bank.

Treasury Notes have maturities from one to ten years. The notes are bearer or in registered form. Interest is paid semiannually.

Treasury Bonds mature in more than 10 years. They constitute the largest segment of our national debt. Treasury Bonds are in bearer or registered form. Interest is paid semiannually. Many of these bonds are callable at par value after five years before maturity on interest payment dates.

References
Cohen, Abby J., CFA, "Investment Planning: The Financial Market Place," National Conference, Denver, Colorado, 1992.
Cohen, Harry D., "Smart Investment Planning," National Conference, Denver, Colorado, 1991.
Economos, Andrew F., PhD, "Global Investment Opportunities," National Conference, Denver, Colorado, 1991.
Golden, Anne B., CFP, "Stocks and Bonds: Defensive Investing," National Conference, Denver, Colorado, 1990.
Markese, John D., PhD, "Investing for Growth and Income," National Conference, Denver, Colorado, 1991.
Perrit, Gerald, W., PhD, " Mutual Funds: Building a Portfolio," National Conference, Denver, Colorado, 1990.
Pond, Jonathan D., CPA, "Financial Planning for the Over 50 Client," National Conference, Denver, Colorado, 1992.
Weisman, Herbert N., D.D.S., CFP, and Weisman, David N., B.A.,

"Retirement Planning for Dentists," *North West Dentistry*, January–February, 1991, pp. 55–56.

20 Common Concerns

During the years that I have done financial planning there are some common concerns many people have. It is interesting that taxes are not one of them. Although paying taxes is not one of life's "joys," most people pay them grudgingly. Anyway, the laws change from year to year making a relevant discussion almost impossible.

Some common concerns seem as follows: How much money will I need to pay for my children's college education? How will I pay for it? and What can I do if I am retired and need more money to maintain my lifestyle? This has been especially true recently. With the decrease in inflation, interest rates have come down dramatically. Health care during retirement seems to cause some concern. At the time of this writing, the Clinton Administration has made some proposals to make sweeping changes in how health care is delivered. Time will tell whether these changes will ameliorate those fears. This section will deal with several areas often not thought about until it is too late—preparation for natural or man-made disasters. Let us look at the problems in order.

Financing College Education

How much is needed to pay for a child's college education? According to an article entitled "College Cash: A Study Guide" that appeared in *Business Week* (September 14, 1992) the cost of tuition at a state institution averages about $6,000 per year. At a private college the cost can run as high as $20,000 per year for tuition alone. Most financial planners believe that you should add 25 percent to this cost for living expenses and other incidentals.

If you have many years for this expense there are numerous ways to plan ahead. First, you can make periodic payments to a growth type of mutual fund. Though there is not usually much in dividends paid, the capital appreciation usually more than offsets the rate of inflation. As college nears, these funds can be either converted into income funds to help pay tuition or gradually sold to pay tuition costs.

A second technique commonly used is to buy a "cash value" life insurance policy such as a universal life policy. When tuition time comes the cash value is "borrowed out" to pay for tuition. As long as there is sufficient cash in reserve to keep the policy in force, the policy remains in effect. If the insured should die prematurely, the payout of the policy would be the face value of the policy minus the cash value borrowed.

Contrary to popular belief, there is a tax implication for this. Part of the funds are borrowing principal, but the other part borrowed is deferred cash buildup. This part is taxable.

United States EE series bonds can be used to pay for tuition. When the proceeds of EE bonds are used to pay for college education, no income tax need be paid on the gains. There are some limitations to this. If you have an income greater than $60,000, this tax benefit gradually diminishes to nothing at $90,000. So buying EE bonds in a child's name has some benefit.

Many individuals make investments in their children's names under the Uniform Gift to Minors Act (UGMA) or Uniform Transfers to Minors Act (UTMA). This is a mixed blessing. While the income generated may be listed under the child's social security number and therefore limit taxes, the assets become the child's legally at age eighteen. This may disqualify the student from receiving student loans. Another question is how many eighteen-year-olds have the maturity to handle large sums of money? Often college money is spent on a new car.

Some people refinance their homes to pay for their children's higher education. While this provides a short-term solution, it is generally not a good idea. The reason is that the new payments are higher and decrease current cash flow needed to be set aside for the parent's retirement. Are your children going to take care of you when you retire? Do you want them to care of you?

If you haven't planned ahead for this expense, there are many student loans and college work programs that are presently available. When President Bush signed the Higher Education Act he open the door to many loans that were previously not available to middle-income parents. Formerly, parents were required to use up to 25 percent of the equity in their home to pay for their children's college education. This requirement was eliminated.

Since 1993, first-year students are able to borrow $23,000 over four years versus $17,250 in federally guaranteed student loans. For graduate students, the amount has been increased to $65,000 from $54,750. These student loans (called Stafford loans) also carry a lower rate of interest. With earlier student loans repayment was delayed until six months after graduation. Loans could be repaid over a ten-year period. Interest was at 8 percent for the first four years and rose to 10 percent in the fifth year. After October 1, 1992, the rates vary. Rates are the rate of interest of three-month Treasury bills plus 3.1 percent.

For those individuals whose income levels are too high, new Stafford loans will be available. The rates will be the same as the regular Stafford loans, but with the new "unsubsidized" loan the student must pay the interest rates from the outset. (Source: Student Loan Marketing Association, Washington, D.C.)

Other financial aid programs are as follows: CW-S (College

Work-Study). This is a federally funded program to furnish needy students with jobs on campus. PLUS (Parent Loans to Undergraduate Students) is another program available. This federal program lets parents borrow up to the entire annual cost of education, less any financial aid, from the bank, with eligibility based on credit worthiness, not financial need. Pell grants are available to high school graduates in financial need who have been out of school for at least seven years. Finally, check with the financial aid administrator's office for any private scholarships that may be available.

How to Increase Your Income in a Low-Interest Environment

Experience with many people, including doctors, attorneys, architects, and other professionals, suggests that they wait too long before thinking about retirement in a meaningful way. Often, living the "good life" plus educating children consumes a high percentage of the family's income. So, not enough is put aside for retirement. Another often-seen scenario is the tendency of many part-time investors to be too conservative with their investments. They look at the current yield only, and not the total return (interest plus growth). The result is that the investments fail to keep up with inflation. In short, purchasing power is lost. Let's look at an example.

John and Mary Smith, ages seventy and sixty-eight respectively, have been retired for the last five years. Before retirement they had accumulated a large portfolio consisting of government securities, certificates of deposit (CDs), and corporate bonds. At the time they retired, interest rates were much higher than they are today. The dividends and interest they received, with Social Security provided them with a comfortable retirement income. Today, many of these fixed income instruments are coming due. Upon renewal, they are finding that current rates of return are mostly less. How can they replace this lost income and still maintain their standard of living? Without it, much of the "good life" that supposedly comes with retirement will disappear. Further, even if inflation continues at the low rate it is today, their purchasing power will continue to erode. In this section I hope to suggest some possible solutions to these problems.

The first technique that can be used to provide additional retirement income is the "Plus One" rule. Though widely known in financial planning circles, it is seldom used by lay people. As mentioned before, this rule says: If a person was to draw out 1 percent interest more than the rate of return that he is getting from his investment, it will take twenty-nine years to use up all of his money. One percent interest may not seem like much money, but (depending on the size of the principal) it can make the difference between a comfortable retirement and a spartan existence. If 2 percent interest above the current yield were used, it would still take twenty years to use all the principal. This is because remaining funds are still drawing interest.

Many older people are afraid to do this because they are afraid that they will outlive their savings. To show that this fear may be unfounded, let us look at our friends John and Mary as an example.

John and Mary have accumulated investments totaling $250,000. With a 9 percent rate of return they would be receiving $22,500 from their investments. This, with approximately $15,000 per year from Social Security, would give them $37,500 total income. If this rate of return should drop to 7 percent their income would be reduced to $32,500. By continuing to draw 9 percent of their principal, it will still take them twenty years to use all their money. Then John will be ninety and Mary will be eighty-eight. A cursory view of mortality tables reveals that this is considerably beyond their life expectancies.

Another idea that can be used to provide additional retirement income is using the cash value of your life insurance. Many seniors have life insurance policies on which they have been paying premiums for years. The rates of interest these policies pay on the cash value is usually very low. If an insured were to "borrow out" the cash value of his life insurance policy and invest the money in an annuity, a lifetime income could be provided for both the husband and wife. Most insurance companies will allow people to borrow up to

90 percent of the cash reserve and still keep the policy in force. It will remain in force as long as the insured pays the interest on the loan. This rate is spelled out in the policy. Older policies have lower rates of interest.

When a person "borrows out" the cash value of his life insurance policy, it is considered a **taxable** loan by the Internal Revenue Service. This is because part of the monies borrowed come from tax-deferred cash accrual. Further, the funds borrowed are still earning interest.

Another means to increase retirement income during time of low interest rates is through "laddering." In order for this technique to be most effective, it should begin when interest rates are high. Before describing laddering, I would like to take a small detour and tell you the differences between how novice and professional investors view things. In that way you will have a better understanding of why laddering works.

During times when interest rates are high, most novice investors will go for the highest current interest for the longest period. On the other hand, the professional investor will look at a yield curve to see where interest rates peak before flattening out. This is the point where he buys a fixed income security. The professional investor knows that it is not always possible to predict the end of rising interest rates, so he will invest smaller amounts at different intervals. The total overall yield will not be the highest yield, but it won't be the lowest either. As an example, let us look at a municipal bond issued from one city. The five-year bond might yield 6 percent. The ten-year bond may yield only $6^1/_2$ percent. The novice investor will buy the ladder bond because it gives him comfort to know that he will be receiving the most dollars regularly. The professional investor will buy the former, figuring that one half percent is not enough reward for the extra five years of risk.

The laddering technique involves buying fixed income investments divided over many different maturities. For example, if bonds are bought over a period of from three to nine years, the risk of lower returns is minimized. After three years, the three-year bond is "rolled over" into a nine-year bond. In this way you can smooth out the bumps of fluctuating returns during the business cycle.

If you are over sixty-two years old, the reverse mortgage is another way to increase income during periods of low interest rates. The good thing about this idea is that you can defer repayment of both principal and interest until the house is sold. Although the idea of borrowing against your home equity and deferring repayment is not new, it has not been widespread. Back in 1989, the Department of Housing and Urban Development (HUD) agreed to insure 2,500 loans through 1991. HUD's intent was to encourage banks to make reverse mortgage loans to seniors. The program continues today.

The amount of income the homeowner receives depends on such factors as the borrower's age, the mortgage interest rates, the value of the property, and the type of plan selected. Because this is a deferred repayment plan it does not depend on what the person can afford to repay. There is a limit of $101,000 on the amount FHA will insure. Also, it is necessary that the applicant meet with an FHA certified counselor to decide their suitability for the program.

As noted above, the reverse mortgage has three options. Option one is known as Tenure. Under this approach the homeowner receives a monthly check as long as he remains in his home. When the house is eventually sold, the proceeds are used to repay interest and principal. Option two is known as Term. Using this plan the homeowner receives a monthly check for a fixed period—usually five to ten years. Then you won't have to sell your home to settle your mortgage, but you will continue to owe interest on what you received. The third option is simply a line of credit. Instead of receiving a monthly check you draw money as needed.

How much will you receive under each option? According to HUD, if you are a seventy-five-year-old and own a $100,000 home free and clear, you could expect the following (assuming a 10 percent interest rate): Under Tenure a person could expect to receive a monthly check for $347. Using a five-year Term plan the individual could receive a monthly check for $790. A ten-year Term plan would yield $496 per month to the borrower. The Line of Credit approach would allow the individual to write loans as needed for up to $39,900.

For more information contact AARP's Home Equity Information Center, 1909 K Street N.W., Washington, D.C. 20049.

Still another method for providing additional income during retirement is known as a life estate. Dr. Albert Lowry, of the Educational Advancement Institute (a real estate school), states that the life estate should be used where the seller wants a guaranteed place to live and is not interested in leaving the property to anyone when he dies. The way it works is as follows: The seller sells his home to a qualified buyer with the provision that he can live in his home for the remainder of his life. In exchange for this provision the price agreed upon is usually considerably less than the fair market value. The seller gets a down payment and a monthly income as long as he is alive. The seller is responsible for the maintenance and taxes. When the seller dies the buyer gets the property free and clear. This is because of the remainderman principal of law. The life estate technique can be used to sell a business as well.

One word of caution is necessary. Before attempting any of the above ideas, be sure to check with a competent attorney or tax advisor.

Charitable Giving

Professional people, small business people, and management people are often perceived by the public as high earners. As such, they are besieged by charities for contributions. Often it is hard to say no. There are some "right ways" and some less advantageous ways to donate to charity. The laws on contributions are complicated, so it is advantageous to understand them.

In 1969, Congress made contributions to qualified charities tax deductible. But not all contributions are equally deductible. For example, Dr. Jones buys a painting for $4,000. After many years it appreciates, and is worth $8,000. Dr. Jones thinks that it would look beautiful in the reception room of the clinic of his dental school. So he donates the painting to the school. How much of a tax deduction does he get? The answer depends on the nature of the charity and the item donated. The dental school, if a state institution, probably qualifies as a charity. The purpose of the school is to train dentists, not learn art history or appreciation. Therefore, Dr. Jones will receive a deduction equal to the amount he paid for the painting ($4,000). If he had donated the painting to a nonprofit art museum, he might have received an $8,000 tax deduction for the same painting. The purpose of the charity must be congruent with the item donated.

For qualified, nonprofit, public charities an individual can deduct up to 50 percent of his income for contributions in a given year. For private foundations the limitation is 30 percent of income in a given year. So you can see that the laws can be very complex. Be sure to check with your tax advisor before making contributions.

Types of Contributions

The easiest kind of contribution is **cash.** Donate cash and get a dollar for dollar tax deduction.

When you donate property, matters get more complex. For example, if you donate **personal property** such as clothes or furniture to the Salvation Army, you can deduct up to $500 without itemizing. For amounts over that amount, all items must be itemized.

For older people (especially those over sixty), an excellent way to give to charity is in the form of the **charitable remainder trust.** This comes in two forms, **charitable remainder annuity trust** and the **charitable remainder unitrust.** In both cases the donor gives appreciated property to a trust for a charity. The trustee then sells the property, if necessary, and invests the proceeds in income-producing securities. The donor and his spouse then receive the income from the securities as long as they are alive. When they die the charity gets the corpus of the trust.

In addition, the donor receives a tax deduction for the present value of the future interest of the trust. This deduction is from an Internal Revenue Service table based on the donor's life expectancy and the rate of return. So for people over sixty the possibilities of getting a substantial deduction is real.

As an example, take a couple sixty-two and sixty years old. They decide that they want to donate $1 million to their church. They own a building worth $1 million. They donate the building to the trust. The trustee sells the building and invests the proceeds into securities paying 7 percent interest. As long as the couple is alive they will receive $70,000 in income. It may be sheltered for up to six years from the tax deduction. For a couple this age, they will receive over $300,000 as a current deduction. The actual amount depends on which kind of trust is set up, but more about that later.

If the couple had held the property for over a year and sold it, they would have had to pay a capital gains tax on the property. This would have left them with less money to donate to their charity and no current income.

What if the couple has a family? If they should want to leave them something, is a charitable remainder trust still usable? The answer is yes. If in addition to the charitable trust the couple also would set up an irrevocable life insurance trust, they could then give to the life insurance trust $10,000 per person, per year, or $20,000 jointly, to pay for life insurance to replace the value of the donated asset.

This does several things. First, the couple donates to their favorite charity an appreciated asset. Second, they get a tax deduction for their donation. Third, they get income from the charitable trust. Fourth, they remove a $1 million asset from their joint estates, thereby saving estate taxes. Finally, they have replaced that asset with an equivalent asset in an irrevocable life insurance trust. This would not be considered part of their estate. This is a win-win situation. The only loser is the tax collector.

As mentioned above there are some differences between the two different charitable remainder trusts. Using a charitable remainder annuity trust (CRAT) the dollar rate remains fixed to the amount at the time the trust is set up. No further additions can be made to the CRAT. These are frequently funded with an insurance annuity.

With a charitable remainder unitrust (CRUT) the rate of interest may be varied from 5 percent to 15 percent. If there is not sufficient dividends and interest to maintain the percentage chosen, the principal may be invaded to make up the difference. Further, additional monies can be added to a CRUT at a later date.

Trusts can be used to do the reverse of the above. In this situation the trust is set up so that the charity gets the income from the trust for years. After that time the corpus (principal) of the trust is returned to the trust creator or his designated beneficiary. This is known as a **charitable lead trust.** This can provide interesting possibilities to save future estate taxes.

The last type of charitable giving is in a **charitable pool trust.** In this situation, a group of investors buy an income property together and donate it to a charitable trust. Each investor receives income from it while he is alive. When he dies, his share of ownership and dividends goes to the designated charity. The investors also receive a current tax deduction of their proportional share of ownership to the charity.

An important note: After 1993, no deduction will be allowed for charitable contributions of $250 or more without substantiation. (This means that canceled checks alone will not suffice.)

Divorce Planning

With "no fault" divorce becoming more common, many people think that all they have to do is sit and divide their common property. This is not so. Having an equitable divorce is different from having an equal divorce. This is because judges consider other things such as lifestyle and each spouse's potential to earn a living.

Much of the information that follows comes from a lecture given by Alan S. Zipp, attorney at law, at the national conference of certified financial planners in 1991. Other information comes from the various worksheets and course outlines for the Certified Financial Planners program of the College for Financial Planning, Denver, Colorado. I mention this only because divorce is a complicated matter. The material contained in the foresaid items is complex. Don't even consider doing this yourself without competent professional help.

The divorce process has three major parts. They are dissolution of the bonds of matrimony, division of marital property, and provisions for the support and care of minor children.

The first step is easy. The second, property division, is more complex. This is because people are supposed to make rational decisions at the time of emotional turmoil. Often there are feelings of resentment, anger, denial, and revenge.

The **property settlement** is a written statement of consent about how marital property should be divided. Once signed by both parties it becomes part of the consent decree. If spousal or child support is needed immediately, a temporary settlement is arranged. This often becomes the groundwork for the final agreement.

Marital property is defined by state statute. Generally, it is all property, however titled, acquired during the marriage by either spouse. Exempted are gifts by third parties, inheritances, property acquired before the marriage, and property excluded by written agreement. Marital property includes all tangible property such as stocks, bonds, furniture, homes, cars, business interests, etc. It also may include intangible property such as the right to receive pension benefits, goodwill of business interests, and the value of a professional degree. In short, everything is fair game.

These assets are listed in a case information statement provided by each party's attorney. Hidden assets are found during the "discovery period." If it is suspected that one of the parties is intentionally trying to conceal assets, the Internal Revenue Service can be called at 1-800-424-3676 to request Form 5406. This is a request for copy A of a tax return.

Once all marital property has been "discovered," each item must be valued and then allocated to the spouses in an equitable manner.

The length of discovery is set by the case management order initiated by the court to put a divorce matter on a time schedule. The order is usually worked out by the party's attorneys. In this way the divorce can be resolved in a timely matter.

Common law property states have an equitable distribution

system by statute or case law. The purpose of this is to get a fair and equitable distribution of marital property based in part by the respective contributions to the marriage. The court decides what constitutes marital property and its value. Sometimes a monetary adjustment is made irrespective of alimony.

The major distinction between common law property states and community property states is that in common law property states property rights accumulate during the marriage. In community property states the court makes this determination. Therefore, in common law property states property is distributed equitably, but *not necessarily equally.*

What happens if a couple gets property in a common law state and then moves to a community property state? Some states, such as Arizona, California, and Texas treat the earlier acquired property as **quasiproperty,** the property had been acquired in the community property state. Other community property states do not recognize this principle and instead go by the rules of the state in which it was acquired.

When the opposite occurs, each spouse retains one half interest in the property acquired while they were married in the community property state.

It is obvious that divorce planning is very complex. It is not in the scope of this book to go into all the complexities and situations possible. Tax planning is one of many considerations. It should be noted that, generally, alimony payments are tax deductible to the payor and taxable to the payee. Child support payments are not tax deductible.

Other issues that should be considered are insurance needs, Social Security benefits, home ownership, legal fees, trust arrangements, credit planning for the non-working spouse, investment planning, retirement planning, estate planning, educational planning, and, finally, emotional planning.

Since divorce is a traumatic event, therapy is sometimes required to deal with emotional issues. Furthermore, the newly divorced person is extremely vulnerable to many demands . Frequently, they will have a tendency to latch onto anyone who will make decisions for him or her. In the December 1992 issue of *CFP Today* (published by the Institute of

Certified Financial Planners), an article appears by Catherine Newton which addresses this issue. In it, she quotes Allen Ungar, author of *Financial Self-Confidence for the Suddenly Single* (Lowell House). He makes these suggestions for people who suddenly find themselves single due to divorce or death:

1. Say no to kids who want to borrow money until you know you what you have and what you can afford to give away.
2. Say no to major purchases and major moves until you've regained your bearings and know your financial reality.
3. Say no to decisions you are making for the benefit of your children unless the decisions benefit you too.
4. Say no to letting someone take over for you. You don't need a surrogate mate.

WEATHERING THE STORM—NATURAL AND MAN-MADE

The article by Catherine Newton just referred to had some other insights into another problem not usually discussed in financial planning but extremely important. What I am referring to is planning for catastrophe.

In the aftermath of Hurricane Andrew and the riots in Los Angeles, many financial planners were interviewed to find out if they could help their clients rebuild their lives quickly. The following lessons were learned:

1. If you have any warning of an impending disaster, keep a few hundred dollars on your person in case your home is destroyed.
2. Keep your car keys and safe deposit key in your pocket.
3. Don't assume that you'll be able to access your ATM. If electricity is out, the machine will be useless.
4. Open an emergency reserve fund at a local bank for quick access; the fund should be large enough to pay for immediate repairs and cover other bills for 1-3 months in case you cannot go back to work.
5. Make a list of your personal property, or record it on video.

6. Put your property list and other important documents in you safe deposit box.
7. When you meet with the insurance adjuster, go in prepared with facts, figures, and documents.
8. Finally, move quickly. Banks will have long lines and limited credit to extend.

References:
Altepeter, Terry V., CPA, "College Funding: Tax Planning Techniques," National Conference, Denver, Colorado, 1992.
Carmichae, Marc, JD, "Charitable Gift-Giving Strategies After the 1990 Tax Act," National Conference, Denver, Colorado, 1991.
Collins, Victoria Felton, PhD, CFP, "Planning Issues and Considerations for Divorce," National Conference, Denver, Colorado, 1991.
Lochray, Paul J., JD, "Using Charitable Gift Annuities in Estate Planning," National Conference, Denver, Colorado, 1992.
Newton, Catherine, "Clients in Crisis," *CFP Today*, December, 1992, pp. 13–15, Institute of Certified Financial Planners.
Ruffell, W. Murray, CFP, "Planning for Your Child's College Education," National Conference, Denver, Colorado, 1992.
Wall, Ginita, CFP, CPA, "Serving Clients After Divorce," National Conference, Denver, Colorado, 1992.
Zipp, Allen, J.D., "Planning for Divorce," National Conference of Certified Financial Planners, 1991, Denver, Colorado.

21 Estate Planning, Wills and Trusts

Introduction to Estate Planning

The previous chapters have laid out a plan for the creation of an estate. The various tools that have been described detail how to create an estate. In this chapter various methods will be discussed regarding how to control it during and after your lifetime.

Estate planning affords the individual an opportunity to preserve control of his property during his life. Furthermore, opportunities are provided to designate who will be the guardians of minor children. In addition, trusts can be used to determine who will inherit your property, and to transfer property after death with minimum delay, publicity, taxes, and transfer costs. By using trusts, after-death management and timed distribution of property for young or disabled dependents can be achieved. Spendthrift trusts can be used for beneficiaries who have difficulty managing their money.

Among the various tools used in estate planning to achieve these ends are wills, trusts, life insurance, joint ownership forms, living wills, letters of instruction, and prenuptial agreements.

PROBATE

Many people are confused about probate. The purposes of probate are to decide the validity of a deceased's will, to identify the deceased's beneficiaries or heirs, to protect the deceased's creditors and determine whether their claims are valid. In addition, probate identifies, collects, and preserves the deceased's assets. It provides a conduit to transfer an estate to the deceased's beneficiaries.

Probate can be expensive. Attorney fees, executor fees, and court costs can eat up a large portion of an estate. These expenses are deductible from a person's taxable estate.

Another disadvantage of probate is publicity. Proceeds are a matter of public record. If it is important to keep matters confidential, other means can be used to transfer property. Some examples of these are the use of joint ownership, living trusts, lifetime gifts, life insurance, annuities, and pension plans.

What happens if someone should die without a will? When a person dies without a will it is said that the person died "intestate." Jointly owned assets pass to the surviving joint owner. If there is no surviving owner, probate is required. Then assets will pass to persons designated by state law.

Trust assets pass to the beneficiaries designated in the trust, and no probate is required.

Lifetime gifts remain with the donee of the gift. Again, no probate is required.

Life insurance, annuities, and pension benefits pass to the beneficiaries named in the contract. Probate is not required if a designated beneficiary survives. If no designated beneficiaries survive, probate is required. Assets then pass to persons designated by state law.

Automobiles solely owned may have their title transferred to the surviving spouse or children without probate. This depends on state law.

All other assets must be probated. These will pass to persons designated by state law.

Wills

Wills are the basic estate planning tool. To be valid, the testator (person making the will) must be of legal age, sound mind, and free of undue influence. The will must be written and signed in the presence of at least two witnesses who are not named in the will. Three witnesses are required in New Hampshire, South Carolina, and Vermont. Witnesses must sign in the presence of the testator and each other.

Some states allow a **holographic** (unwitnessed) will. The will must be dated, in the testator's own handwriting, and signed at the end of the will. This can be useful when there is not enough time or opportunity for a formal witnessed will.

Wills can designate primary and contingent beneficiaries. They can disinherit survivors (except spouses). In Louisiana, children are also exempt. Wills can be used to bequeath real or personal property, forgive debts to the testator, make charitable gifts, postpone or condition gifts, and establish testamentary trusts. These trusts are effective at death. It is common for the **personal representative,** sometimes known as the executor, and guardians and conservatives to be named in a will. Finally, the trustees of the trusts created in the will should be named. As long as conditions contained in a will are legal and not against public policy, defamatory, or libelous, the will will be considered valid.

Note: Anatomical gifts and funeral and burial instructions should not be contained in a will. This is because wills are not usually read until after the funeral. A separate letter of instruction is more useful for this purpose.

Wills can be changed without redoing the whole declaration by using a **codicil.** These too must be witnessed like an original will. Any time the testator changes his mind about the disposition of assets or guardianships, he may make a codicil directing the change.

Wills can be revoked for any of the following reasons: A new will that revokes the previous wills; a will purposely destroyed by the testator or at his direction; divorce or annulment revokes any disposition to the former spouse unless the will expressly provides otherwise.

Wills should be stored in a safe place, free from danger of fire, theft, misplacement, or loss. Its whereabouts should be known to some survivor or confidant. A will may be deposited for safekeeping in the probate court in the county of the testator's residence. The testator may retrieve the will during his lifetime. After death, the will is publicly opened and retained by the court.

Though some people keep their wills in a safe deposit box, remember that these are sealed when the bank becomes aware of the testator's death.

JOINT OWNERSHIP

Joint tenancy is a form of co-ownership whereby two or more "joint tenants" own property. When one dies, the surviving owner automatically acquires the deceased partner's interest. **Tenancy in common** is different from joint tenancy in that the deceased's interest passes to his heirs or the surviving beneficiaries noted in the will.

The advantages of joint ownership are that it is inexpensive to establish and simple. Usually, it avoids probate. Sometimes it may insulate a property from claims of creditors.

The disadvantages of joint ownership are that it is irrevocable without the consent of the other party. This could result in loss of control of the property during the owner's lifetime. It could unintentionally disinherit a person or give a property to someone for whom it was not intended. Furthermore, it could expose the property to claims of the joint owner's creditors.

From the estate tax point of view, when spouses own property jointly, one half of the jointly owned property is included in the estate of the first joint owner who dies. With all others, full value of the property is included in the estate of the first joint owner to die, unless it can be proven that the surviving joint owner contributed to the acquisition or maintenance of the property.

Even if all property is jointly held, a will is still needed. This helps overcome the possibility of simultaneous death during a common disaster. Furthermore, when the joint owner dies, the other becomes the sole owner. Wills help dispose of missed or overlooked property. It can dispose of wrongful death proceeds or insured proceeds (if the designated beneficiaries precede the second owner). Guardianships of minors can be named in a will.

TRUSTS

A trust is created by *transferring* property to a trustee who manages and distributes it to specified beneficiaries pursuant to a trust agreement.

There are several different kinds of trusts. They are revocable living trusts (created separate from your will), testamentary trusts (created in your will), and short-term trusts (e.g., Clifford trust and Spousal Remainder trusts) that are no longer useful since the Tax Reform Act of 1986.

Trusts can be created for any legal purpose. Some common uses for trusts are as follows: to manage assets for a spouse or minor; to bypass a spouse to avoid or minimize estate taxes; to insulate assets from creditors; to protect inheritance from malpractice liability; to avoid probate; to avoid conservatorship; to time or postpone distribution to children or spendthrifts; to protect handicapped persons who are qualified to receive SSI or other government benefits (this is done with a **Kraven trust**); to protect marital assets from passing to a second husband (or wife) rather than to children of the marriage.

As an example of how trusts may be used in estate planning, let us use the last purpose. The estate tax laws allow for an unlimited transfer of property from one spouse to another at time of death with no tax liability. (The will must say you wish to take advantage of this law. It is not automatic.) At first glance this looks wonderful. A more thoughtful view of this reveals two problems. First, when the second spouse dies, the estate may be left with a huge tax liability. Second, if the second spouse should remarry, there may be pressure by the new spouse to spend that money for all kinds of purposes.

Consequently, no money may be left for the children from the first marriage.

How can trusts solve this problem? The solution is as follows: First a **credit shelter trust (family bypass trust)** is set up in the will. This is known as a **Trust B**. Each person is allowed a $600,000 exemption by law before estate taxes need to be paid. So $600,000 worth of assets are designated by the will to fund this trust. The assets in this trust can be used to pay the surviving spouse or other family members an income. The trust dissolves when the surviving spouse dies. Assets are then distributed to remaining beneficiaries.

Another trust is also set up in the will. This is known as either a **Trust A, or a Qualified Terminal Interest Property (QTIP)** trust. Both trusts qualify to receive the remaining unlimited marital deduction. Also, both trusts can pay the surviving spouse income from the trust. There are some important differences.

Using a Trust A the surviving spouse can designate who ultimately receives the corpus of the trust. She/he can also make unlimited withdrawals from the trust for any purpose. So it becomes easier for a spouse in a second marriage to pressure the surviving spouse to invade the trust for their needs.

When a QTIP trust is used the grantor of the trust designates who ultimately receives the corpus of the trust. Further, a Crumey provision is added to restrict emergency withdrawals to 5 percent or $10,000, which ever is less. This affords the grantor more control of his funds.

When the surviving spouse dies, another $600,000 exemption is allowed. So when using trusts it is possible to shelter $1.2 million from the tax collector. This will save $385,600 in estate taxes.

POWER OF ATTORNEY

There are many situations where some objectives of a trust can be achieved at lower cost and less hassle by power of attorney. This is a document by which you appoint another person to act as your agent to manage your property during your lifetime. The person appointed need not be an attorney. The powers granted can be general in nature or limited to a specific transaction. (An example of this might be to sign a deed while you are out of state.) A power of attorney is revoked by disability or incompetency unless it is a **durable** power of attorney. Most states now allow this action.

Durable power of attorney is often used when someone becomes mentally or physically disabled. It avoids the embarrassment and inflexibility of a court appointed guardian or conservator. This may also save some expense.

The power of attorney is automatically revoked at death. Therefore, it cannot be used as a probate device.

LIFE INSURANCE REVISITED

In a previous chapter, life insurance was covered in some detail. In this chapter, some uses of life insurance as an estate planning device will be discussed.

As an estate planning tool, life insurance can serve many purposes. One of these is providing funds for survivors to buy out the interest in a partnership or personal corporation. This is particularly useful because it avoids the need to liquidate or include mortgage assets to accomplish the buyout.

By providing liquidity for an estate, money becomes available for payment of debts taxes and other settlement costs. Remember, estate taxes must be paid within nine months of death.

Insurance is often used to enlarge an estate. It also helps to insure adequate support for dependants. This is particularly common in situations where the "breadwinner" dies prematurely and leaves a family. Life insurance can make the difference in the family's future lifestyle.

Life insurance can be used as an investment in the creation of a personal retirement fund. The cash values build up on a tax-deferred basis over the years. When retirement arrives, discreetly "borrowing" out of the cash value while keeping the policy in effect can provide money during this time. If the policy is cashed in, there will be income tax on the interest and dividend portion of the cash received. This is the same as the insurance "loan" except no insurance remains in force.

It is important to understand that if the decedent owns his life insurance policy, the proceeds *are* included in his taxable estate. This can be avoided by simply transferring all incidence of ownership to the spouse or an irrevocable life insurance trust. If no spouse is available, anybody can own the policy (but they must pay the premiums).

When designating beneficiaries, it is also important to specify an alternative beneficiary. This avoids problems if the first beneficiary preceedes you in death. Furthermore, if your policy designates your estate as the beneficiary, the insurance proceeds will be subject to probate.

LIVING WILL

A living will is a document that instructs others, if you are in a health situation where there is no reasonable expectation of recovery from physical or mental disability, not to begin "heroic" measures. Currently living wills are recognized in forty-three states.

In order for a living will to be valid, it must be dated, notarized, or signed and witnessed by two people who will not benefit from your death (and are not employees of your doctor).

Free information and forms are available from the Right to Die Society, 250 West 57 Street, New York, NY 10107. Telephone them at (212) 246-6973. Since they are nonprofit, they would appreciate a donation.

LETTER OF INSTRUCTION

A letter of instruction is just what it says. It tells your survivors whom you owe money, what you owe, and what to do about it. If you want specific funeral arrangements, this is a good place for them. If you want to inform your survivors about your ideas or philosophies, this is the place for them. Letters of instruction are not legally binding, but they do provide a guide to others as to how to settle your affairs.

Store one copy of the letter of instruction with your will, give your attorney another, and keep a third copy where you think others will find it.

MANAGING PROPERTY OF MINORS

The Uniform Gift to Minors Act (and Uniform Transfers to Minors Act) allows gifts of personal property to be given to any adult as a custodian for a minor. Custodial property must be used for the benefit of the minor without regard to the parent's resources. All income and principal *must* be turned over to the minor at age eighteen.

Many parents who use this conduit fail to realize that these assets legally become the child's to use as they see fit. They lose control. How many eighteen-year-olds have the maturity to handle large sums of money? There have been many instances where the child has used this money for a great vacation rather than college (as the parent wished). Furthermore, when these assets are in the child's name, they may not qualify for college loans or scholarships for which the applicant must show need.

Income tax implications are as follows: for minors under fourteen, income up to $1,200 is taxed at the minor's low rate. All income over $1,200 is taxed to the child but at the parent's rate. (Fortunately, there is a $600 exemption and the personal exemption of $2200 that shelters much income.) For minors fourteen and over, all income is taxed to the minor at his rate.

Estate tax implications are as follows: If the minor dies before the payout, the fund is included in the minor's estate. There is one exception to this, if the donor makes himself the custodian and dies before the minor reaches majority.

There is no gift tax as long as the gift from the donor is $10,000 or less in a given year. ($20,000 if the donor's spouse consents to the gift.)

When the gift is made, it should be registered as "John Doe, as custodian for Mary Doe."

UNIFIED FEDERAL GIFT AND ESTATE TAX

The Unified Federal Gift and Estate Tax is a tax on lifetime and deathtime transfers of property. The tax includes all property and assets that the decedent had an interest in at the time of death. This includes solely owned and jointly owned property, assets held in a revocable living trust, and life insurance proceeds.

Deductions from the taxable estate include debts, expense of last illness and burial, cost of settling estate, and the value of all charitable bequests.

Exemptions from gift and estate taxes include the following: Annual gifts of $10,000 ($20,000 if donor's spouse consents) to any number of donees, estates of $600,000 or less, and the value of all assets passing to a spouse.

Some ways in which estate taxes can be reduced are as follows: set up a program of lifetime gifting—gifts of assets are likely to appreciate in value; transfer ownership of life insurance policies; use the unlimited marital gift and estate tax deductions—splitting estates between husband and wife, and using bypass trusts, when the estates exceed $600,000, can be a very effective means of reducing estate taxes.

COMMON ESTATE PLANNING MISTAKES

Proper estate planning can save your family thousands of dollars and much heartache. In the following section ten common estate planning mistakes are discussed.

MISTAKE 1: IMPROPER USE OF JOINTLY HELD PROPERTY

Jointly held property is sometimes called the "poor man's" will. This is because at the death of one of the parties, the property automatically passes to the survivors. Although this avoids probate, it can create a potentially large tax liability. This is particularly true were the surviving joint tenant is not a spouse. In this situation, the entire property will be taxed in the estate of the first party to die—except to the extent the survivor can prove he or she contributed to the property. When the surviving partner dies, it becomes part of his or her estate and will be taxed again. Furthermore, because property held in joint tenancy automatically passes to the survivor, it may negate wishes expressed in the will of the deceased owner. Finally, property held jointly cannot be used to fund a credit bypass trust. This can result in payment of unnecessary estate tax.

Mistake 2: Improperly Arranged Life Insurance

The most common mistake when using life insurance is having the policy owned by the party who is insured. This causes the proceeds of the life insurance to be included in the estate of the insured. In turn, this makes the proceeds subject to estate tax. This can be avoided by transferring ownership of the policy to the beneficiary (such as a spouse) at least three years before death. Better yet, the ultimate beneficiary should purchase the policy, using their money, from the policy's inception.

Another common mistake is making the insurance payable to a beneficiary before he is legally, physically, or emotionally able to handle it. This is common when minor children are named beneficiaries. Instead, a trust should be created for their needs until they are legally able.

Often, there is inadequate life insurance on the "breadwinner" of the family, or the key person in a business. This, too, can result in a severe financial and emotional hardship for the beneficiaries.

Another problem that frequently arises is the lack of enough beneficiaries named in a life insurance policy. Sometimes the primary beneficiary has died. If no contingent beneficiary is named, the laws of the state apply.

Sometimes a situation arises when the owner of a policy on another person's life names someone other than the owner as beneficiary of the policy. For example, a mother owns the policy on her husband and names the children as beneficiaries. At the husband's death, she is in effect making a gift to her children. This would be subject to gift taxes applied against her estate.

Speaking of named beneficiaries, the owner's "estate" is often named as a beneficiary. This needlessly subjects these funds to probate, estate taxes, and claims of creditors against the estate. This can be the basis for an attack on the will itself.

If an interest in a life insurance policy is transferred for any valuable consideration in money or money's worth, the proceeds lose their tax free status.

Where a spouse is required, as part of a divorce settlement to purchase life insurance or as part of the settlement, the premiums are not deductible. A better approach would be to increase the alimony payments enough to allow the spouse to purchase the policy. Alimony payments are deductible.

One other caveat: if a corporation names someone other than itself or its creditor as the beneficiary on the life of a key employee, the IRS will argue that these are dividends and subject to ordinary income tax. This can be important where split dollar insurance is used for a key employee. When this is done, be sure there is a written agreement specifying all the terms.

MISTAKE 3: LACK OF LIQUIDITY

Most people have no idea how much it will cost to settle their estates or how quickly taxes must be paid (nine months from the date of death). Suddenly, the estate is forced to sell valuable assets for sale prices in order to pay these expenses. Be sure there is adequate cash available for these purposes. Below is a checklist for this purpose.

Checklist:
1. Federal Estate Taxes
2. State Death Taxes
3. Federal Income Taxes (including taxes on pension distributions)
4. State Income Taxes (including taxes on pension distributions)
5. Probate and Administration Costs
6. Payment of Debts
7. Maintenance of Family
8. Payment of Specific Cash Requests
9. Funds for Continued Operation of a Family Business
10. Generation Skipping Transfer Tax (55%)
11. Excise Tax on Excess Pension Accumulations (15%)

Mistake 4: Choice of Wrong Executor

While the purpose of picking an executor may seem simple (at first glance), it really can be complex. Consider that the executor must collect all assets, pay all bills, and distribute the remaining assets to the beneficiaries without conflict of interest. This is a time-consuming job that is often done without compensation. Sometimes the named executor has neither the time nor the inclination to do this. Sometimes the executor may not live in the same state. If the person who is appointed executor does not get along with family members, chaos can result.

Mistake 5: Will Errors

Perhaps the biggest mistake is dying without a will. This forces the state to decide who gets what. Dying intestate has already been discussed.

Other common will errors include failing to update them when family events such as births, adoptions, marriages, divorces, etc. occur. Wills should also be updated when there are major changes in the tax laws. When a testator moves to another state, the will should be changed to reflect the laws of that state. Finally, when there are major changes in circumstances of either the testator or the beneficiary (such as an increase or decrease in income), updating the will should be considered.

Mistake 6: Leaving Everything to Your Spouse

Many people believe that because there is an unlimited marital deduction they should leave everything to their spouse. This is unwise for several reasons. First, although estate taxes are avoided at the death of the first spouse, there is a big wallop in estate taxes at the death of the second. The rate is 37 percent on the amount in excess of $600,000 and can reach up to 60 percent as a maximum.

The solution to this is setting up a credit bypass trust. This not only shelters $600,000 of assets but can provide income and security to the surviving spouse.

The second reason leaving everything to a spouse is unwise is that the surviving spouse often has little experience handling large amounts of money. Insurance statistics have shown that most people go through large sums of "unearned" money within two or three years.

If a family business is involved, the surviving spouse frequently does not have the knowledge or experience to run it. The same may be true for real estate holdings.

Mistake 7: Improper Distribution of Assets

An improper distribution of assets occurs when the wrong person gets the wrong assets. An example of this was discussed above (leaving everything to the spouse). There are other examples. For instance, assets can be divided in an equal but not necessarily equitable manner to beneficiaries. Say there are three surviving children with different incomes or different physical problems. One may be brilliant, the second may be average, and the third may have a learning disability. Leaving equal distributions to each may not provide the same comfort level to each child.

The solution may be to create a **"sprinkle trust"** to provide extra income or principal to a child who needs it in a given year.

Another example of wrong asset distribution might be leaving a car to someone who no longer drives or to a very young minor. This is not as uncommon as you might think. I have seen wills where a spouse who was legally blind was left an expensive car. This occurred only because the will was not updated when the health change occurred.

Mistake 8: Failure to Stabilize and Maximize Value

Many doctors and other small business owners fail to stabilize their practices or businesses due to economic shock. This can be caused by death or disability of key personnel. This problem can be minimized by purchasing office overhead expense insurance, disability insurance, and by making buy-sell agreements. In the latter, the purchase price, or at least the mechanism for pricing the practice or business, should be spelled out in writing. Often these are funded with a life insurance policy.

Wills should name the business beneficiary and a contingent beneficiary as a backup to continue the business operations.

Mistake 9: Lack of Adequate Records

Lack of adequate financial records can be a nightmare to the executor. Though many of them, such as tax returns etc., can be duplicated, it can cost the estate much unnecessary expense.

Mistake 10: Lack of a Strategic Game Plan

Many lay people do not think of their estates as very complicated. So they attempt to save money by doing their own estate planning. As has been pointed out in this section, this can result in unnecessary estate taxes and distribution of assets to unintended beneficiaries. The bottom line is: educate yourself as much as possible regarding what is available and seek professional help to implement your plans. Monitor your plans on at least a semi-annual basis.

References

Atlas, Theodore B., Esq., "The Use of Trusts in Estate Planning," National Conference, Denver, Colorado, 1990.

Barwich, Donna G., CPA, "Understanding the Use of the Living Trust," National Conference, Denver, Colorado, 1991.

Black, Howard, JD, CFP, ChFC, "Planning in Anticipation of Incapacity," National Conference, Denver, Colorado, 1991.

Cady, Donald F., JD, LLM, LLU, "Estate Planning and Survivorship Life Insurance Policies," Denver, Colorado, 1990.

Leimberg, Stephan R., Kandell, Stephen N., etc., *The Tools and Techniques of Estate Planning*, 7th edition, National Underwriter, Cincinnati, Ohio, 1988.